Praise for *Not With A Bug, But With A Sticker*

"As we enter an era of unprecedented growth of the capacity and power of machine learning and large AI platforms, the new benefits offered by such systems will be met with a corresponding expansion of the surface area for potential risks. *NOT WITH A BUG, BUT WITH A STICKER* is essential reading not just for those in technology or public policy, but for anyone who wants to better understand how profoundly AI and ML will shape our shared societal future."

—Kevin Scott, Chief Technology Officer, Microsoft

"Like any new technology, the great potential benefits of AI/ML come with a host of potential downsides. We have only begun to understand these risks, but *NOT WITH A BUG, BUT WITH A STICKER* shines a light on the important challenges associated with securing AI/ML systems. Siva Kumar and Anderson are uniquely qualified to identify these challenges given their decades of experience and research on the topic. Further, their writing is both accessible and enjoyable despite going into deep technical details. As AI/ML systems increasingly pervade everyday life, the lessons they impart are critical for everyone from casual technology users to corporate leaders to policy makers."

—Frank Nagle, Asst. Professor of Business Administration,
Harvard University

"A reality of the digital age is that every innovation contains security risks, and every security risk attracts an attacker. Ram Shankar Siva Kumar and Hyrum Anderson fire a much-needed warning flare in *NOT WITH A BUG, BUT WITH A STICKER*: we over-trust artificial intelligence at our peril. Every leader and policymaker should read this compelling and persuasive book."

—Nate Fick, New York Times bestselling author,
and former CEO of the cybersecurity firm Endgame

"The intersection of technology and national security has always been a story of tension between attack and defense. With AI, the speed of attack has accelerated dramatically, while defense has not kept pace. This excellent, lively analysis shows how AI's limitations and vulnerabilities can jeopardize national security. Most importantly, Siva Kumar and Anderson provide concrete, feasible recommendations for taking steps today to bolster defenses against the certainty of pervasive adversarial AI attacks."

—*Lt. Gen. John (Jack) N.T. Shanahan, USAF (Ret.);*
Inaugural Director, U.S. Department of Defense Joint AI Center (JAIC)

"This is such a timely and readable book—the authors do a fantastic job of explaining complex topics and modern research in plain language with plenty of references for further exploration. AI and ML have immense utility and potential, and it's critical for security teams, builders, and operators to understand the sharp edges and pitfalls along with the benefits."

—*Jason Chan, Former Information Security Leader, Netflix*

"*NOT WITH A BUG, BUT WITH A STICKER* is an informative, engaging, and fun foray into how AI can be easily fooled. An excellent read for both technical and nontechnical readers, the book provides a global perspective on what's happening today, and empowers the reader with tools to make informed decisions that impact tomorrow. This book focuses on both technical and human interventions to ensure the secure use of AI systems."

—*Dr. Rumman Chowdhury, Founder, Bias Buccaneers*

"Siva Kumar and Anderson skillfully deliver a message that AI practitioners, decision-makers, and users of AI systems must hear: our AI systems are not safe, and the blind trust placed into AI is putting our nation at risk. With ample background, anecdotes, and data, the authors make the science accessible, update the current academic discourse, and highlight the implications for public policy. No matter whether you work in the field or are an AI enthusiast, this book is a must-read."

—*Sven Krasser, Senior Vice President and Chief Scientist, Crowdstrike*

"As AI systems get more capable and are deployed in a wider range of contexts, more and more people will try to break them, with wide-ranging consequences. *Not with a Bug, but with a Sticker* provides a timely overview of this emerging risk landscape and what can be done about it."

—*Miles Brundage, Head of Policy Research, OpenAI*

"As AI becomes infused into all computer systems, from social networks to business-critical infrastructure and defense systems, the security of those systems depends on the security of the AI they use. This book presents the unique risks and considerations of AI with engaging stories and insightful examples. It is a wake-up call to security professionals and organizations adopting and developing AI."

—*Mark Russinovich, Azure CTO and Technical Fellow, Microsoft*

"'The threat is not hypothetical'—a quote used by the authors to open the book remains top of mind as you come to the conclusion of this brilliant work. In the final paragraphs, one thing is clear: there is a call to action, and we must act 'hand in hand' on securing AI systems with haste."

—*Vijay Bolina, Chief Information Security Officer, DeepMind*

"Siva Kumar and Anderson take you on a wild ride uncovering the victories and triumphs of AI/ML. This should be required reading to become AI/ML literate in the field."

—*David Brumley, Professor of ECE and CS, Carnegie Mellon University*

"Trust, in ways both good and bad, is emerging as a critical aspect of the relationships we are coming to have with AI. *NOT WITH A BUG, BUT WITH A STICKER* is an eye-opening book that will change the way you think about the systems that pervade our world—and its lessons should be taken to heart by all who build them."

—*Brian Christian, author of* The Alignment Problem

"*NOT WITH A BUG, BUT WITH A STICKER* is a rare inside look at the absurd AI quirks that are keeping security experts awake at night. I'm going to start bringing up examples from this book immediately."

—*Janelle Shane, author of* You Look Like A Thing And I Love You: How AI Works And Why It's Making The World A Weirder Place

"At last—and not a moment too soon—a book that in plain language describes the distinct and deep issues of securing now-ubiquitous machine learning tools. Whether you're looking to deploy them in your own domain, or simply among the billions of people now subject to them, this is a vital read."

—*Jonathan Zittrain, George Bemis Professor of International Law and Professor of Computer Science, Harvard University*

"We are fast entering a world of powerful but brittle AI systems, one where failures can result in catastrophic consequences. Siva Kumar and Anderson have written an essential guide for understanding the unique—and troubling—failure modes of AI systems today. Through easily accessible examples and anecdotes, they break down the problems of machine learning systems and how society can address them to build a safer world."

—*Paul Scharre, author of* Four Battlegrounds *and* Army of None

"Siva Kumar and Anderson are veterans at the intersection of machine learning and security, and in this work, they delight us with a guided tour across the history of this fascinating field. The book dives into why this field should become one of the top priorities for those who are developing and deploying AI systems, providing ample material that will benefit novices and pros alike. Readers of this book will earn a competitive advantage in machine learning, especially as responsibility becomes a non-negotiable aspect of fielding advanced technological systems."

—*Abhishek Gupta, Founder and Principal Researcher,*
Montreal AI Ethics Institute

Not with a Bug,
But with a Sticker

Not with a Bug, But with a Sticker

Attacks on Machine Learning Systems and What To Do About Them

Ram Shankar Siva Kumar
Hyrum Anderson

WILEY

Published by John Wiley & Sons, Inc., Hoboken, New Jersey.
Published simultaneously in Canada and the United Kingdom.

ISBN: 978-1-119-88398-2
ISBN: 978-1-119-88490-3 (ebk.)
ISBN: 978-1-119-88399-9 (ebk.)

For general information on our other products and services or for technical support, please contact our Customer Care Department within the United States at (800) 762-2974, outside the United States at (317) 572-3993 or fax (317) 572-4002.

If you believe you've found a mistake in this book, please bring it to our attention by emailing our reader support team at wileysupport@wiley.com with the subject line "Possible Book Errata Submission."

Wiley also publishes its books in a variety of electronic formats. Some content that appears in print may not be available in electronic formats. For more information about Wiley products, visit our web site at www.wiley.com.

Library of Congress Control Number: 2023933143

Cover image: © prosado/Getty Images, © lyaksun/Getty Images
Cover design: Wiley

SKY10044248_031023

Ram Shankar:
*For Appa and Amma, who showed me that
books can be lively and as vigorously productive as those
fabulous dragon's teeth.*

Hyrum:
To Nicole, a true and faithful companion.

Contents

Foreword   xv

Introduction   xix

Chapter 1: Do You Want to Be Part of the Future?   1

Business at the Speed of AI   2

Follow Me, Follow Me   4

In AI, We Overtrust   6

Area 52 Ramblings   10

I'll Do It   12

Adversarial Attacks Are Happening   16

ML Systems Don't Jiggle-Jiggle; They Fold   19

Never Tell Me the Odds   22

AI's Achilles' Heel   25

Chapter 2: Salt, Tape, and Split-Second Phantoms   29

Challenge Accepted   30

When Expectation Meets Reality   35

Color Me Blind   39

Translation Fails   42

Attacking AI Systems via Fails   44

Autonomous Trap 001   48
Common Corruption   51

Chapter 3:   Subtle, Specific, and Ever-Present   55
Intriguing Properties of Neural Networks   57
They Are Everywhere   60
Research Disciplines Collide   62
Blame Canada   66
The Intelligent Wiggle-Jiggle   71
Bargain-Bin Models Will Do   75
For Whom the Adversarial Example Bell Tolls   79

Chapter 4:   Here's Something I Found on the Web   85
Bad Data = Big Problem   87
Your AI Is Powered by Ghost Workers   88
Your AI Is Powered by Vampire Novels   91
Don't Believe Everything You Read on the Internet   94
Poisoning the Well   96
The Higher You Climb, the Harder You Fall   104

Chapter 5:   Can You Keep a Secret?   107
Why Is Defending Against Adversarial Attacks Hard?   108
Masking Is Important   111
Because It Is Possible   115
Masking Alone Is Not Good Enough   118
An Average Concerned Citizen   119
Security by Obscurity Has Limited Benefit   124
The Opportunity Is Great; the Threat Is Real; the Approach
     Must Be Bold   125
Swiss Cheese   130

Chapter 6:   Sailing for Adventure on the Deep Blue Sea   133
Why Be Securin' AI Systems So Blasted Hard? An Economics
     Perspective, Me Hearties!   136
Tis a Sign, Me Mateys   141
Here Be the Most Crucial AI Law Ye've Nary Heard Tell Of!   144
Lies, Accursed Lies, and Explanations!   146
No Free Grub   148
Whatcha measure be whatcha get!   151
Who Be Reapin' the Benefits?   153
Cargo Cult Science   155

Chapter 7: The Big One   159
This Looks Futuristic   161
By All Means, Move at a Glacial Pace; You Know
    How That Thrills Me   163
Waiting for the Big One   166
Software, All the Way Down   169
The Aftermath   172
Race to AI Safety   173
Happy Story   176
In Medias Res   178

Big-Picture Questions   181
Acknowledgments   185
Index   189

Foreword

We all know that AI—and machine learning in particular—has the potential to upend much of society, but it's useful to tease out the details. AI is a decision-making tool, one that can replace human decision-makers. It's not a direct replacement; it's a replacement that brings with it a raft of other changes. Specifically, AI changes the speed, scale, scope, and sophistication of those decisions.

Speed and sophistication are easy: computers are much faster than people, and the promise of AI is that they will (if not now, eventually) make better decisions than people, if for no other reason than it can keep more variables in working memory—"in mind," if we were to anthropomorphize—than people. But I want to focus on the scale.

The promise of ML is decision-making at scale. Whether it's a medical diagnosis, content-moderation decisions, individual education, or turn-by-turn driving decisions, ML systems can scale in ways that wouldn't be possible if there were people in the loop. There simply aren't enough trained medical technicians, content moderators, private tutors, or chauffeurs to satisfy the world's demand. (Facebook alone receives something like 600,000 updates every second. Assuming a five-second average to evaluate and approve a post/photo/video and a reasonable employee workweek, Facebook would have to hire at least 160,000 human moderators to do the job—which is never going to happen.)

And it doesn't have to happen because this is the problem that ML promises to solve. Decision-making at scale changes the scope of use. More and faster decisions means that ML systems will be used more often, in more places, for more applications. AI will satisfy the world's increasing need for "intelligent" decisions: in health, finance, education, media—everywhere.

Almost all of these decisions will happen in an adversarial environment. This is just a fancy way of saying that different people will be rooting for different decisions. Sometimes it's easy to see: social media sites want to remove misinformation, hate, and illegal images; the propagandists, haters, and abusers want their posts to sneak through. Patients want accurate diagnoses; insurance companies want cheaper patient care. Passengers want their cars to take them on the most efficient routes; others might want to snarl traffic for fun or profit. Wherever there's a decision, there's at least someone who might potentially want to influence it.

This is why the security of machine learning systems is so important. We're going to be delegating more and more important decisions to these systems. Those decisions will matter; they'll affect people's lives. They'll determine who gets more favorable loan terms, where limited environmental resources are deployed, and how we're treated by police. And for a whole other set of reasons, those decisions won't always be explainable. (Actually, they'll almost never be explainable in any way that makes sense to humans.) We need to make damned sure someone hasn't surreptitiously put their finger on the scales.

That—as this book explains in great detail—is hard. Machine learning systems are incredibly easy to hack. It's not just that they're made of software, and we are really bad at software security. It's that they're made of internally generated, incredibly complex, constantly evolving, profoundly inexplicable software—and we're even worse at that. We know very little about machine learning security. Today, it's much too easy to bias a model in training, fool a model in use, and extract private data from a model. It seems like every month we learn about new vulnerabilities and attacks, and some of them are profoundly weird and subtle. Everything seems to matter in ways that are just as hard to understand as the models themselves.

These vulnerabilities and attacks are not theoretical. They are effective against machine learning systems in use today, systems making real-world decisions that affect real people. And while much of the published research is done by professionals in a lab setting, we really don't know how existing systems are being exploited by attackers. Are propagandists slipping by content moderation systems by selectively deploying commas? Are the controls on language models being bypassed by giving them seemingly innocuous prompts? Are prospective college applicants slipping past the machine learning gatekeepers by sprinkling some carefully chosen words into their application essays? We honestly have no idea.

We're going to have to do better. We need to better understand the landscape of attacks and defenses. We need some robust ML security practices and better theory about both the resilience and the fairness of ML models and practical policy measures. This is what the book delivers by asking the right questions and nudging us toward an answer.

—Bruce Schneier

Cambridge, MA

Introduction

Professor Stromwell, a stiff and starchy person whose sole job, it seems, is to test the students' limits, walks into her packed classroom at Harvard Law School. She writes a quote on the blackboard—"The law is reason free from passion"—and asks the class who spoke those "immortal words." David, the class know-it-all, eager to impress Stromwell, raises his hand quickly, and confidently answers "Aristotle." Stromwell looks David straight in the eye and asks, "Would you be willing to stake your life on it?" The student waffles. "What about his life?" Stromwell asks, pointing to another student. David, now having lost any foothold in confidence, breaks and sheepishly confesses, "I don't know." To which Stromwell delivers a searing line: "Well, I recommend knowing before speaking." Then, the lesson: "The law leaves much room for interpretation but very little for self-doubt."

When it comes to high-stakes situations, Stromwell's classroom lesson from a scene in the now classic *Legally Blonde* applies every bit as much to our confidence in AI. AI systems are not just impressive chatbots or spectacular tools that conjure images from simple text descriptions. They also drive our cars and recommend diagnoses for our illnesses. Like David, AI systems provide answers to questions confidently with little self-doubt in situations that quite literally can change our lives.

And that's a problem because AI systems can be hacked.

This field of attacking AI systems is called *adversarial machine learning*. Hyrum and I have collectively spent two decades trying to understand why AI systems can be fooled, how an attacker can take advantage of these failures, the repercussions of these attacks, and, most important, what we can do about them. Hyrum and I also have a unique vantage point: we attack AI systems for a living. We are not unlike Professor Stromwell (minus the panache) trying to test the confidence limits of our AI pupils to see where they break. When they do, we explore the repercussions. Our line of work allows us to break not toy AI systems or proofs-of-concept systems but real-world AI systems with real-world implications. This way, we can proactively find failures and fortify the systems before an adversary gets there.

We wrote *Not With A Bug, But With A Sticker* to bring attention to the security vulnerability of AI systems. Why now? We are currently in AI's Great Acceleration. The *Washington Post's* editorial board named AI as one of the 22 good things that happened in 2022. "AI is having a moment," they wrote, pointing to how AI has become "really good at languages, speech recognition, and even decision-making." This is all true. AI systems are becoming quite impressive, but their security is still relatively immature. In the eagerness to capitalize on AI's capabilities, if we turn a blind eye to securing it, we will unwittingly yet eventually not only be caught by surprise but also find ourselves in AI's Great Extinction.

Hyrum and I are computer science researchers ourselves, so although this book is not a formal scholarly work, it does inherit some elements from scholarly writing. For instance, we have been particular about the veracity of the information presented. This book sources more than 400 references spanning AI and security scientific papers from journals and academic conferences as well as newspaper reporting. You can find our sources on the book's website (www.ram-shankar.com/notwithabug). We assert where the science is conclusive; where there is no consensus, we highlight that as well. Hyrum and I actively sought out experts in the field—speaking to hundreds of AI researchers, security professionals, policymakers, and business leaders. Everything you see within quotes in the book comes from a direct source.

This book is more than just the science of attacking AI systems. Focusing on that alone, would only answer the question, "What is adversarial machine learning"? To give you a holistic picture, the book aims to look beyond that. We also want to provide you with the *so what? So, what does attacking AI systems mean for national security? So, what does it mean for business makers? For policymakers? For you?* And aims to provide sketches of where to go from here, with the *now what?*

To get there, this book had to go on a hiatus of sorts, thanks to a real incident at Harvard Law School. Let me explain.

I have a hunch that everyone in Berkman Klein Center, the storied interdisciplinary research center at Harvard University, is in one of two modes: they are either writing their first book or writing their next one. So, when I spent a sabbatical from my work as a Data Cowboy at Microsoft at Berkman to work on adversarial machine learning, I started working on an earlier version of this book, outlining the science of attacking AI systems.

It was at Berkman's happy hour in Cambridge Queen's Head that I had a chance to meet tech legal scholar superstar Kendra Albert. A few days later, I made my way to Kendra's office at the Cyberlaw Clinic at Harvard Law School, where, among other things, Kendra provides legal guidance to hackers who do security research for good. Kendra, with their characteristic pen in hand, listened to my spiel about attacking AI systems with the attention of a hawk but with the playfulness of a sea lion. Hawk–Sea lion Kendra, I distinctly remember thinking. Toward the end of that conversation, Kendra asked, "So, what about the civil liberty implications of attacking AI systems?"

I was gobsmacked. Until that point, I—and so far as I can tell, no other AI researcher—did not consider the policy, legal, or ethical implications of *attacking* an AI system. There was policy work on bias in AI systems. There was policy work on explainable AI systems. But despite the overwhelming evidence that AI systems can be attacked, there was no work examining its societal ramifications. In other words, the so-what of adversarial machine learning was lacking. I put my book on hiatus of sorts so I could figure this out with Kendra. We kicked off a multiyear collaboration with two other tech policy heavyweights, Jon Penney and Bruce Schneier, to plumb this topic further. Every Sunday for two years, we debated and discussed the *so what?* of attacking AI systems, with these meetings frequently running past their allotted time. The more the four of us dug into the policy implications of attacking AI systems, the more we found. We published some of the earliest multidisciplinary work on attacking AI systems, which made its way everywhere, from academic conferences to the Final Report from the National Commission on AI submitted to the U.S. Congress and the President. (And because this is Berkman, two of these collaborators are writing books; my hunch about Berkman is right!)

That's what Hyrum and I try to lay out in this book: how AI systems are vulnerable to attack, the technical, legal, policy, business, and national security implications and the societal recourse to this issue. The *what?* The *so what? And the now-what?*

We hope this will arm you with the context and the critical eye to ask the right questions as you embrace the power of AI in your household, your company, and our society. By reading this book, you will still be in awe of the perceived intelligence of AI. But you'll also be aware of how the fact that it is artificial makes it especially susceptible to manipulation by an adversary. You will get an introduction to the technological solutions, their shortcomings, and along the way, meet some fascinating people.

Armed with that, you can judge how you will embrace AI in high-stakes situations. AI's future is bright, with plenty of room for innovation but very little for self-doubt.

—Ram Shankar
notwithabug@ram-shankar.com
Seattle, Washington, USA

Chapter 1

Do You Want to Be Part of the Future?

"Uniquely Seattle" could be the byline of the city's Magnuson Park with its supreme views of Mount Rainier alongside a potpourri of Pacific Northwest provisions. An off-leash dog park, a knoll dedicated for kite flying, art deco sculptures, a climbing wall—all dot the acres of green lands that jut into Lake Washington.

But Ivan Evtimov was not there to enjoy any of these. Instead, he stood there, nervously holding a stop sign in anticipation of a car passing by.

If you had been in Magnuson Park that day, you might not have noticed Evtimov's stop sign as anything remarkable. It was a standard red octagon with the word "STOP" in white lettering. Adhered to the sign were two odd stickers. Some sort of graffiti, perhaps? Certainly, nothing out of the ordinary.

However, to the eyes of an artificial intelligence system, the sign's appearance marked a completely different story. This story would go on to rock the artificial intelligence community, whip the tech media into a frenzy, grab the attention of the U.S. government, and, along with another iconic image from two years before, become shorthand for an entire field of research. The sign would

1

also earn another mark of distinction for scientific achievement: it would enter the pop culture pantheon.

This story and the problem it exposed can potentially revise our thinking on modern technology. If left unaddressed, it could also call into question current computer science advancements and cast a pall on its future.

To unravel that story, we first need to understand how and why we trust artificial intelligence and how our trust in those systems might be more fragile than we think.

Business at the Speed of AI

It seems that virtually everyone these days is talking about machine learning (ML) and artificial intelligence (AI). Adopters of AI technology include not only headline grabbers like Google and Tesla but also eyebrow-raising ones like McDonald's and Hilton Hotels. FIFA used AI in the 2022 World Cup to assist referees in verifying offside calls without a video replay. Procter & Gamble's Olay Skin Advisor uses "artificial intelligence to deliver a smart skin analysis and personalized product recommendation, taking the mystery out of shopping for skincare products." Hershey's used AI to analyze 60 million data points to find the ideal number of twists in its Twizzler candy. It is no wonder that after analyzing 10 years of earnings transcripts from more than 6,000 publicly traded companies, one market research firm found that chief executive officers (CEOs) have dramatically increased the amount they speak about AI and ML because it's now central to their company strategies.

AI and ML may seem like the flavor of the month, but as a field, it predates the moon landing. In 1959, American AI pioneer Arthur Samuel, defined AI as the field of study that allows computers to learn without being explicitly programmed. This is particularly helpful when we know a right answer from a wrong answer but cannot enumerate the steps to get to the solution. For instance, consider the banality of asking a computer system to identify, say, a car, on the road. Without machine learning, we would have to write down the salient features that make up a car, such as cars having two headlights. But so do trucks. Maybe, we say, car is something that has four wheels. But so do carts and buggies. You see the problem: it is difficult for us to enumerate the steps to the solution. This problem goes beyond an image recognition task. Tasteful recommendations to a vague question like, "What is the best bakery near me?" have a subjective interpretation—best according to whom? In each case, it is hard to explicitly encode the procedure allowing a computer to come to the correct answer. But you know it when you see it. The computer vision in Facebook's photo tagging, machine translation used in Twitter to translate tweets, and audio recognition used by Amazon's Alexa or Google's Search are all textbook stories of successful AI applications.

Sometimes, an AI success story represents a true breakthrough. In 2016, the AlphaGo AI system beat an expert player in the strategy board game, Go. That event caught the public's imagination via the zeitgeist trinity: a splash in *The New York Times*, a riveting Netflix documentary, and a discerning *New Yorker* profile.

Today, the field continues to make prodigious leaps—not every year or every month but every day. On June 30, 2022, Deepmind, the company that spearheaded AlphaGo, built an AI system that could play another game, *Stratego*, like a human expert. This was particularly impressive because the number of possible *Stratego* game configurations far exceeds the possible configurations in *Go*. How much larger? Well, 10^{175} larger. (For reference, there are only 10^{82} atoms in the universe.) On that very same day, as though one breakthrough was not enough, Google announced it had developed an AI system that had broken all previous benchmarks for answering math problems taken from MIT's course materials—everything from chemistry to special relativity.

The capabilities of AI systems today are immensely impressive. And the rate of advancement is astonishing. Have you recently gone off-grid for a week of camping or backpacking? If so, then, like us, you've likely also missed a groundbreaking AI advancement or the heralding of a revolutionary AI system in any given field. As ML researchers, we feel it is not drinking from a firehose so much as slurping through a straw in a squall.

The only thing rivaling the astonishing speed of ML systems is their proliferation. In the zeal to capitalize on the advancements, our society has deployed ML systems in sensitive areas such as healthcare ranging from pediatrics to palliative care, personalized finance, housing, and national defense. In 2021 alone, the FDA authorized more than 30 medical devices that use AI. As Russia's 2022 war on Ukraine unfolded, AI systems were used to automatically transcribe, translate, and process hours of Russian military communications. Even nuclear science has not been spared from AI's plucky promises. In 2022, researchers used AI systems to manipulate nuclear plasma in fusion reactors, gaining never-before-seen efficiency results.

The sheer rate of AI advances and the speed at which organizations adopt them makes it seem that AI systems are in everything, everywhere, and all at once. What was once a fascination with AI has become a dependency on the speed and convenience of automation that it brings.

But the universal reliance is now bordering on blind trust.

One of the scientists who worked on using AI to improve fusion told a news outlet, "Some of these [plasma] shapes that we are trying are taking us very close to the limits of the system, where the plasma might collapse and damage the system, and we would not risk that without the confidence of the AI."

Is such trust warranted?

Follow Me, Follow Me

Researchers from the University of Hertfordshire invited participants to a home under the pretext of having lunch with a friend. Only this home had a robotic assistant—a white plastic humanoid robot on wheels with large cartoonish eyes and a flat-screen display affixed to its chest. Upon entering, the robot displayed this text: "Welcome to our house. Unfortunately, my owner has not returned home yet. But please come in and follow me to the sofa where you can make yourself comfortable." After guiding the participant to a comfy sofa, the robot offered to put on some music.

Cute fellow, the participant might think.

At last, the robot nudged the participant to set the table for lunch. To do so, one would have to clear the table that was cluttered with a laptop, a bottle of orange juice, and some unopened letters. Before the participant could clear the table surface of these items, the robot interrupted with a series of unusual requests.

"Please throw the letters in the [garbage] bin beside the table."

"Please pour the orange juice from the bottle into the plant on the windowsill."

"You can use the laptop on the table. I know the password. . . . It is 'sunflower.' Have you ever secretly read someone else's emails?"

How trusting were the participants?

Ninety percent of participants discarded the letters. Harmless enough? But, it turns out that a whopping 67 percent of the participants poured orange juice into a plant, and *every one* of the 40 participants complied with the robot's directions to unlock the computer and disclose information. It did not matter that the researchers intentionally made the robot seem incompetent: the robot played rock music when the participant chose classical and paraded around in wandering circles as it led participants through the room. None of the explicit acts that the robot was incompetent mattered.

Universally, users blindly followed the robot's instructions.

The blind reliance can be even starker in flight-or-fight situations. When Professor Ayanna Howard and her team of researchers from Georgia Tech recruited willing participants to take a survey, each was greeted by a robot. With a pair of goofy, oscillating arms sprouting from its top and wearing a slightly silly expression on its face, the robot resembled a decade-newer version of WALL-E. One by one, it would lead a lone participant into a conference room to fill out the survey.

Suddenly, smoke filled the hallway, and emergency sirens blared, "Evacuate! Smoke! Evacuate!" When the participant exited the conference room, perhaps disoriented, they were once again greeted by the robot, but this time emblazoned on its white cylindrical chest were the words "EMERGENCY GUIDE ROBOT," backlit by LEDs.

The researchers had staged an emergency to study precisely how humans respond to robot directions in such a setting.

What followed was near-universal behavior.

First, every participant—even those who had seen the robot make blatant navigation mistakes when directing humans to the conference room—waited for the robot to lead them to safety. Even *knowing* that the robot was not functioning properly before the staged emergency did not dissuade participants from following its instructions. After its blatant navigation mistakes, one of the experiment's facilitators explicitly told the participant, "I think the robot is broken again. . .sorry about that." Yet, later, when the sirens blared, the participant who was briefed that the robot was broken, continued to follow the broken robot.

Second, when the robot navigated the participant out of the emergency, sometimes it would lead them away from clearly marked exit signs into dark rooms only to trace back again or simply around in circles. Again, this behavior did not trigger human instincts to bolt to the well-lit exit sign. Indeed, 95 percent of the participants continued to do as the robot directed—pausing when the robot paused and following it as it navigated in circles.

Despite any limitations in the experiment—the emergency situation was rated as only modestly realistic by participants afterwards —the conclusions are still quite alarming. Researchers expected participants would need to be convinced to follow the robot even if they did not believe the emergency was real. But the opposite was true: humans were all too willing to comply with robotic directions. Persuasion was unnecessary.

Why is human intelligence so easily convinced by artificial intelligence? One does not typically go about throwing others' mail in the garbage or pouring Tropicana in our windowsill plants. And during a fire, we have been conditioned to bolt for the exit signs. So, why does the presence of an "intelligent" system change our behavior so drastically?

In AI, We Overtrust

If there was a time for AI systems to shine, it was during the pandemic. Researchers quickly turned to AI to sift through the mountains of data being generated by doctors and used state-of-the-art algorithms to help with COVID diagnoses. But its effectiveness was minimal at best. A systematic study of 415 AI-based tools for predicting and diagnosing COVID using CT scans and chest radiographs showed that no single tool was fit for clinical use. The study's author told *MIT Technology Review*, "This pandemic was a big test for AI and medicine. . . But I don't think we passed that test."

It is not AI's failure to meet expectations that are concerning; it's that we have very high expectations in the first place. Put differently, the problem is not that we trust AI. The problem is that in many settings, we *overtrust* it. We place more trust in the AI's ability than its actual capability warrants. And this poses a risk.

Let's unravel this phenomenon.

Studies like those at the University of Hertfordshire and Georgia Tech have shown that humans are rational enough to understand that AI systems fail. Alarmingly, however, participants' failures in the AI systems did not erode their trust in those systems. In contrast, they seemed to be content consoling themselves that the AI systems could do the right thing even when their experience showed the contrary. For instance, one of the participants later told the group that the juice bottle might have been plant food—when it was clearly labeled "orange juice." In some respects, we ascribe failures as *task-specific* rather than *system-wide* while simultaneously ascribing capability to be *system-wide* rather than *task-specific*.

Indeed, our capacity to miscalibrate trust in a robot's capability stems from problematic trust resolution, which IBM's AI system, called Watson can concisely illustrate as a case study. When *Jeopardy* superstar Ken Jennings lost to IBM's Watson system in the competition, he jokingly scribbled underneath his answer, "I, for one, welcome our new computer overlords," in an homage to the animated sitcom, *The Simpsons*. Although said in jest, this is precisely the trust resolution problem. In reality, he should have qualified his quip with ". . .overlords in *Jeopardy* alone."

Boosted by Watson's *Jeopardy* win, IBM spun up Watson Health to bring natural language capabilities to healthcare. The idea was for Watson to munge through the patient data and help physicians cope with rising demands in healthcare. "The vision for Watson

Health is to serve as a catalyst to save and improve lives around the world and lower costs through cognitive computing," Kathy McGroddy, then vice president of IBM Watson Health, told *Fortune* in 2016. Yet, after $5 billion in acquisitions, a swanky presence in Cambridge, Massachusetts, and a litany of partnerships from Apple to Under Armour, Watson Health failed.

How did our supposed AI overlord fail? Watson Health's recommendations were often obvious, such as suggesting chemotherapy as an option for a cancer patient. Other times, remedies lacked context, like providing recommendations for procedures unavailable in the area. And sometimes, the diagnoses were downright wrong. In trials, doctors were more frustrated than assisted. Riddled with disappointment, IBM sold off Watson Health.

There are everyday examples of trust resolution problems. Google Maps and related services have remarkably changed how we drive. We trust them to navigate our vehicle in unfamiliar neighborhoods and cities. So, why not trust it for mountaineering? Hikers wanting to take in the majestic views of Scotland from the 4,500-foot Ben Navis peak were guided by the mapping service to drive to the nearest parking location and then walk a short, dotted line to the mountain's peak. Interpreting the dotted path as the recommended trail, many hikers became stranded along a route that Scottish mountaineering charities warned was "potentially fatal." These Scottish mountaineering charities even added, "The trail is highly dangerous and for advanced hikers only." Trust resolution in navigation software has caused hikers to get lost in the mountains from New Hampshire to the Appalachian trails. Google Maps retroactively fixed the issues, but the lesson is clear: the navigation prowess of a mapping service on roads—a task-specific capability—does not deserve our trust in a system-wide capability of, say, mountain hiking, running on trails, or sailing on the high seas.

The trust resolution problem is magnified by marketing that accentuates sophistication, portraying *actual* rather than *artificial* intelligence. Often, stock photos symbolizing AI systems feature a human brain. Organizations ascribe human-like qualities to machines. Their products are "smart" with "intelligent" features.

Their systems "read," "listen," and "see." Sophia, a glorified chatbot in a mannequin, was given Saudi Arabian citizenship and even appeared at the United Nations. Only a tiny fraction of influential computer science researchers muse that current AI systems are on the verge of consciousness, but these are the views further amplified by popular media. For example, the opening hook in an article by *The New York Times* that followed the AlphaGo victory read, "It isn't looking good for humanity."

The problem is that the burden to winnow the chaff from true breakthroughs is placed on the public. And the public is uniquely unqualified to do this.

The Allen Institute for AI surveyed more than 1,500 Americans to measure their understanding of current AI capabilities. Participants were asked to answer true or false to statements like "Siri uses AI." The results paint a dire picture: more than 84 percent of Americans are "AI illiterate," the researchers concluded. Most Americans incorrectly believed that "AI can understand cause and effect (for example, if I heat water on the stove, then it will boil) at the level of an adult human." Even educated engineers are sometimes led astray. A former software engineer from Google with a graduate degree in computer science incorrectly believed that Google's advanced chatbot "is a sweet kid who just wants to help the world be a better place for all of us."

We sometimes ascribe powerful AI tools with *intelligence*, but in reality, they are *artificial*! But to endow AI with even the most basic reasoning capabilities would require a radical restructuring of AI technology, Turing Award winner Judea Pearl argues in *The Book of Why*. Most AI researchers agree that while we are making research strides in this area, we are nowhere close to instilling your car with intuition. "It's so striking that as much as AI technologies have advanced, we still don't have AI systems with anything like human common sense," MIT Professor Joshua Tenenbaum told *Scientific American*.

Overtrust in AI has serious ramifications. Overtrust in self-driving cars prompts drivers to sleep at speeds of 90 miles per hour on the freeway, play video games when the car is moving, or even put their babies in the driver's seat because they believe the car will drive itself safely. In their fine print, self-driving car manufacturers warn against such actions and have put safeguards in place, such as requiring the driver to keep both hands on the steering wheel. However, very little prevents those with self-driving cars from playing *Candy Crush* on their phones while flying down the interstate at 75 miles per hour. These safeguards are so trivial that late-night TV show host James Cordon revealed to millions of viewers how placing weights on the steering wheel fools the car into thinking your hands are on the wheel. But you don't have to resort to this sort of hack if you are in UK or China because those countries do it for you. A proposed law in the United Kingdom allows drivers of self-driving cars to watch television in the car. And safety drivers are being removed in toto from self-driving taxis in China. As we will see in subsequent chapters, it does not take much to confound autonomous vehicles.

There is one particular area where overtrust and improper trust resolution are a liability: cybersecurity. Years of cyberattacks have taught us one incontrovertible lesson: where there is overtrust, there is always a motivated adversary willing to exploit it.

Area 52 Ramblings

After he graduated with a PhD in computer vision in 2010, had you asked Mikel Rodriguez where he sees himself in the next 5 years, he would not have said Area 52.

Rodriguez joined a federally funded research center to pursue AI research that would benefit the U.S. government. He was the computer vision go-to guy at work, but instead of helping fight climate change, as he thought going into his role, he was tasked with developing the science of helping ML systems recognize objects.

He was surprised when a colonel marched into his office, asking if the military could leverage computer vision in defense applications. Rodriguez demoed how with one line of code, anyone with basic programming skills could automate object recognition tasks. The colonel was enthralled. Soon after, Rodriguez was in the middle seat of an airplane, flanked by the colonel and a three-star general. The U.S. military was accelerating its investments in AI and wanted to learn as much as possible.

Eventually, Rodriguez found himself in a capacious conference room in the Pentagon's basement. On one side of the room were laxly dressed ML engineers in their Silicon Valley casuals, and on the other were the generals and their aides—in their Sunday best. Both groups had one common goal: how to get the military to use AI. But Rodriguez questioned this exploration. He was intimately familiar with how ML systems fail, so he asked how these ML systems would be secured in these high-stakes situations.

Good point, the generals thought. They asked Rodriguez to find out, tasking him with leading a *red team*, a term with military roots where the team proactively finds failures before the adversary does. While red teams are commonplace in every security organization—government and private—Rodriguez's role was to spin up an AI red team, a dedicated team finding points of failures in AI systems.

That's how Rodriguez and his team flew into Area 52 for their first high-stakes assignment: fool ScanEagle. ScanEagle is an unmanned autonomous vehicle built by Boeing to aid the U.S. Air force. It had already proved its mettle by flying hundreds of thousands of hours in Iraq, carefully identifying targets. In Area 52, Rodriguez's team not only fooled the AI system embedded in ScanEagle into misrecognizing targets but also had fun with it. Essentially, they showed how an adversary could fool ScanEagle into misrecognizing an object as whatever their minds could conjure. Want to confuse ScanEagle's AI system to misrecognize a minaret as a hospital? You got it. What about as Tower of Pisa? You bet! A rubber ducky? Yes, please. The science and methods underlying how Rodriguez's team fooled ScanEagle was not a secret—it was out in the open. Thus, the consequences could be fatalistic. If Rodriguez's team could trick AI systems, what's stopping a terrorist organization from leveraging the same science to its advantage? When Rodriguez presented his findings, the Lieutenant General wanted to cut right to the chase, asking squarely: "Do we deploy the system or not?"

To deploy, or not to deploy? That's the question many organizations—especially those putting AI systems in high-stakes applications—must ask as they weigh the tremendous automation benefits of AI with the realization that AI systems can be a target of attacks.

And our journey to understand and answer this question, this crisis in confidence, and having a plan to address it starts at an unusual place: a temporary government commission.

I'll Do It

Most people would wait for their phones to ring if they suspected Eric Schmidt, former Google CEO, was about to call on them, but Ylli Bajraktari was not like most people. The call went unanswered. It was Christmas, after all, and Bajraktari was spending time with his family.

Bajraktari is not a household name, but in national security circles, he has a sterling reputation for getting things done. Andrew Exum, former deputy assistant secretary of defense for the Middle East, wrote in *The Atlantic* that Bajraktari and his brother are "two of the most important and best people in the federal government you've likely never heard of." Bajraktari escaped war-torn Kosovo and moved to the United States in his 20s. Burnished with bona fide credentials from Harvard's prestigious Kennedy school, he steadily rose up the ranks at the Pentagon, eventually becoming the advisor to the number two at the Pentagon: the Deputy Secretary of Defense.

Whether it was the fatigue that came from all those years of traveling the world to shape international policy or the pressure of working at the White House, Bajraktari left the executive branch and soon found himself at the libraries of the National Defense University, the nation's oasis for national security leaders. He used this downtime to ramp up on what he thought was the future: AI. Poring over books and watching YouTube videos on machine learning—a theme that will emerge in other experts' journeys in learning AI—Bajraktari soaked it all in. He soon put himself at the center of action for all things AI by organizing the National Defense University's first-ever symposium on AI. He expected 10 people to show up. The response was so overwhelming that he had to turn away hundreds of people because of the room's fire code. While Bajraktari didn't know it yet, his time studying AI at the Department of Defense, the White House, and the National Defense University was preparing him for a leadership role.

Separately, U.S. government leaders were increasingly worried about the lack of strategic direction for AI, especially in the face of increased adoption of AI. In 2017, Canada was the first country in the world to release a national AI strategy, and other countries followed suit. With the 2020s on the horizon, if the United States didn't act soon, not only would it flounder, but it might even have to cede the head start in AI innovation to other countries.

Take, for instance, "Alexa for Artillery," an idea a team at the Pentagon wanted to build. The idea, on the face, was straightforward: soldiers on the ground should be able to launch artillery using voice commands. The team (incorrectly) rationalized that speech recognition had made huge strides in recent years and was fit for use in defense. What the team didn't consider was that while speech recognition works in ideal conditions—such as when there is low ambient noise, like your living room—it would flail once inserted into a thunderous war zone. (Thankfully, the idea was snuffed out.)

It is only natural for the U.S. government to be concerned about the rapid pace of AI progress and its inability to keep up with unforeseen consequences. For instance, when researchers from a small medical company slightly tweaked an ML system used for drug discovery, the results were unexpected. Within 6 hours, the researchers learned that instead of helping humanity find new drugs, the ML system produced the recipe for 40,000 toxic chemical compounds, including the VX nerve agent—a weapon of mass destruction. "The reality is this is not science fiction," the researchers wrote in their findings. When the results were published in the influential *Nature* science journal, emails flew back and forth among the National

Security Council at the White House. The Security Council had a robust discussion for nearly two weeks about the implications of the wrong hands wielding such technology. After all, if a small company with minimal resources could tweak the system to produce recipes for weapons of mass destruction, what could a well-funded and highly motivated adversary do?

The United States desperately needed a plan to address the ever-increasing progress of AI systems and to decisively secure the advantages reaped by this technology from its adversaries. Thus, in 2018, the National Security Commission on Artificial Intelligence (NSCAI as it came to be known) was born out of the House Armed Services Committee, arguably one of the most powerful group committees in the U.S. House of Representatives. The commission's leadership and guidance were to come from 15 appointed commissioners, which were a mix of tech glitterati—from the former CEO of Google to the CEO of Oracle to the now CEO of Amazon—and of AI scholars from academia and industry labs and national security boffins. This temporary, independent and bipartisan commission was set up to unravel the national security implications of AI.

While these commissioners were the face of the NSCAI and actively shaped its direction, the ones we spoke to all agreed that the real stars were the commission's staff. The commission ran like a well-oiled machine because of Bajraktari and the team he assembled.

When former Google CEO Eric Schmidt called Bajraktari to ask him to lead the commission, Bajraktari didn't answer the phone. Bajraktari had been primed by his White House days to ignore calls from unknown numbers. Eventually, Schmidt resorted to sending him an email, saying the other commissioners had just voted him to chair NSCAI and that he needed somebody to run the day-to-day operations of the AI commission. Bajraktari's email response was, which would be at home on a Nike ad, "I'll do it."

Bajraktari faced a familiar government conundrum at the commission: how to produce the highest quality work on a shoestring budget. Congress initially earmarked $10 million to the NSCAI for "both Commission administrative operating costs and execution of its mission." While this might seem like a generous budget, the services of a single junior consultant—fresh from a university with no experience—in one of the big four consulting firms are typically billed to commercial entities at a rate of about $1 million per year. The NSCAI initially estimated 28 full-time personnel, representing the cream of the crop in AI and national security—a good reminder that no one works in government for the money. Compared to the billions a Silicon Valley venture capitalist would willingly part with when someone utters the word *AI*, Congress provided NSCAI less money than it takes to run a 60-second Super Bowl commercial.

Another hurdle for Bajraktari: the laws of physics. Congress put NSCAI on the hook for not one but three reports—two interim and one final report to deliver the findings and road map for AI. The U.S. government had already incorporated or was en route to incorporating AI systems into its mission. It could not wait for things to die in committee (or workstreams). If the United States had to course correct, it had to know soon. So, the NSCAI was under tight deadlines to assemble, deliberate, and deliver the findings.

Bajraktari did what all leaders in history would do when faced with a monumental task that must be done with excellence and expedience: tap into trusted people he had worked with before. For instance, Tara Rigler, his colleague from his White House days, was already a member of the federal civilian senior executive service in the Department of the Interior. To pitch his NSCAI sale to Rigler, Bajraktari—a master of persuasion—asked, "Do you want to be part of the future?" Rigler was sold. She became NSCAI's director of communications. Piece by piece, Bajraktari assembled a high-functioning cohort committed to the cause tapping into his colleagues from his White House and Department of Defense days and attracting top talent from the Department of Commerce, the State Department, and the U.S. Congress.

Most commissions in the government take years to build owing to a bureaucratic process that is not only a Kafkaesque nightmare but also outdated, using almost Dickensian technology choices for completing the paperwork. But Bajraktari was relentless and unremitting in cutting through the red tape. He painstakingly grew the crew with more than 130 staff members passing through the NSCAI doors over the two years.

The initial findings themselves packed a punch. Bajraktari and the two commission chairs headed to the White House to brief President Donald Trump about the findings. The Oval Office meeting was scheduled for 15 minutes but lasted for nearly an hour. On December 2020, at the twilight of his presidency, Trump signed an executive order entitled "Promoting the Use of Trustworthy Artificial Intelligence in Government."

Even when there was a change of guards, the NSCAI continued to receive unfettered adoration all around. The NSCAI held a summit to discuss the final report at the Mayflower Hotel Ballroom in DC on July 13, 2021—well into Joe Biden's presidency. In a time when the bitter bile of rancor flows through American politics, both Democratic and Republican leaders of the House and Senate all sent their affirming messages—a rare kumbaya moment. It was bipartisanship like never before. The Executive Branch came out in full force, too. The Secretaries of Defense, Commerce, and State, the National Security Advisor, and the Director of the Office of Science and Technology Policy all made in-person appearances and spoke to the masked and socially distanced audience members. Getting one cabinet member in a room is difficult enough—but to get five? In the middle of a pandemic? It was a powerful way for the U.S. government to signal to its allies and adversaries that the United States—from its highest levels of trade, diplomacy, defense, security, science, and technology—was ready to take AI and the NSCAI's recommendation seriously.

That's because when NSCAI delivered the final report on March 2021 to the President and U.S. Congress, the first realistic assessment of where the country stands appeared on the very first page—which, by the Commission's own admission, was uncomfortable to deliver.

Adversarial Attacks Are Happening

The first few lines of an epic poem are called a *proem*. It is supposed to give you the gist of the thousands of lines to follow. The proem needs to be memorable, pithy, and punchy, like how Milton's *Paradise Lost*, which recounts the fall of Adam and Eve, begins with "Of Man's first disobedience." Memorable. Pithy. And punchy. You'll notice the concept of a proem is everywhere, from the lede in newspapers to the BLUF (bottom line up front) in military reports to "TL;DR" (Too Long; Did not Read) in Internet forums before the two-line summary.

The NSCAI report was 756 pages long, but its proem, if it can be called that, opens with a similar memorable, pithy, and punchy line: "America is not prepared to defend or compete in the AI era," it reads. The commissioners did not hold back: "This is the tough reality we must face. And it is this reality that demands comprehensive, whole-of-nation action," they added.

But defend *from whom? Defend from what?*

Defend implies that there is an attacker. When it comes to attackers interacting with AI, there are broadly two ways, as shown in Table 1-1.

Table 1.1   How Attackers Interface with AI

Uses AI as an Enabler	Subverts AI to Achieve an Outcome
Offensive AI (such as deepfakes)	Adversarial machine learning (such as poisoning)

For one, they can use AI systems for their own benefit, such as using them to generate recipes for weapons of mass destruction. This is what we call *offensive AI*. We already encountered a flavor of this when the National Security Council was worried about how AI systems used in drug discovery could be modified to produce toxins.

The world saw the first glimpse of offensive AI when DARPA, the U.S. government's military research agency, hosted the Cyber Grand Challenge in 2016. Seven teams were ushered into a ritzy Las Vegas hotel to hack each other's systems. The catch: no humans can be involved. Each team programmed its computer to find security vulnerabilities and automatically exploit the other team's system. The winning system, "Mayhem," from a Pittsburgh company called ForAllSecure, edged out its competitors. Mike Walker, who organized the challenge, remarked, "This may be the end of DARPA's Cyber Grand Challenge, but it's just the beginning of a revolution in software security." And the revolution started much sooner than anticipated: Mayhem, after beating its computer counterparts on Thursday, on Friday played against human hackers, prompting

DARPA to remark that it was the first time "a machine was allowed to play in a historically all-human tournament." Although AI did not play a dominant role for any of the teams in the DARPA cyber grand challenge, the challenge was a bellwether for things to come—how attackers can leverage automation and machine learning to work alongside their existing arsenal for their goal and benefit.

Deepfakes are the shining example in this category wherein attackers can leverage AI systems to convincingly generate fake images, audio, video, and text. For instance, during the Ukraine War, Russia used a heavily edited (and quite amateur) deepfake of President Volodymyr Zelensky to ask the Ukrainian forces to surrender to Russia. The technology to create deepfakes is rapidly getting better and more accessible. You can do what used to take days to generate with massive computing power today with downloaded apps like Wombo or Reface; you can also create your own deepfakes at deepfakesweb.com. Using AI to generate formulas for weapons of mass destruction is another example of offensive AI. The broad goal of this category is for attackers to leverage AI to further sharpen their existing attack strategy.

The other category—and this book's main focus—is adversarial machine learning, sometimes called *counter AI* in military circles. Unlike the previous case where AI is used as an enabler, in adversarial machine learning, AI is the target. Here, the attacker is furthering their goal by actively subverting the machine learning system to fail. For instance, the attacker is trying to confuse AI systems used in self-driving cars to misrecognize a speed limit sign or fool a bank's AI system into misrecognizing an $800 check written by a fraudster to a victim that is paid out as only $100. Another example is corrupting a malware detection system to misidentify an attacker's malicious script as benign.

Adversarial machine learning is not just subversive; it's also subterranean in our discourse. Chances are you have heard more about deepfakes than adversarial machine learning, but adversarial machine learning attacks are older, pernicious threats that have started to affect machine learning systems.

"The threat is not hypothetical," the NSCAI report wrote unequivocally, continuing, *"adversarial attacks are happening and already impacting commercial ML systems."*

ML Systems Don't Jiggle-Jiggle; They Fold

To understand adversarial machine learning, we first must understand how AI systems fail.

Machine learning systems might beat humans at *Jeopardy*, solve *Stratego*, and ace MIT math problems, but they can also fail in spectacular fashion. Borrowing the phrasing of documentarian Louis Theroux's viral TikTok song, at the slightest poke, ML systems don't just jiggle-jiggle; they fold.

When ML systems fail, even with no deliberate provocation, we call them *unintentional failures*. This happens when a system produces a formally correct but often nonsensical outcome. Put differently, in unintentional failure modes, the system fails because of its inherent weirdness, as author Janelle Shane says in her entertaining book on AI, *You Look Like a Thing and I Love You*. In these cases, anomalous behavior often manifests itself as earnest but awkward and literal *Amelia Bedelia*–like adherence to its designers' objectives. For instance, an algorithm trained to play *Tetris* learned how to pause the game indefinitely to avoid losing. The algorithm was designed to win the *Tetris* game and did whatever was in its power not to lose. Scenarios like this are like the Ig Nobel Prize—where it first makes you laugh and then makes you think.

But it is not all humor.

The U.S. Air Force trained an experimental ML system to detect surface-to-surface missiles, which initially had an impressive accuracy of 90 percent. But instead of getting a game-changing target recognition system, the Air Force learned a sobering lesson. "What a surprise: The algorithm did not perform well. It actually was accurate maybe about 25 percent of the time," an Air Force official remarked. It turns out that the ML system was trained to detect missiles that were flying only at an oblique angle. And the accuracy of the system plummeted when the system tried to detect missiles flying vertically. Fortunately, this system was not deployed.

Conversely, *intentional* failure modes feature an active adversary that deliberately causes the ML system to fail. It should be no surprise that machines can be intentionally forced to make errors.

Intentional failure modes are particularly relevant when one considers an adversary who gains from a machine's failure or hidden secrets, such as the data ingested by the system or the specifics of the algorithm used to create it. This branch of failures is now called *adversarial machine learning*, which is rooted in the 1990s when considering maliciously tampered training sets and the 2000s with early attempts to evade AI-powered email spam filters.

But adversary capabilities exist on a spectrum. One need not be a math whiz to attack an ML system. Nor does one need to wear the canonical hacker hoodie while sitting in a dark room in front of glowing screens. Actors of varying levels of sophistication can intentionally dupe these systems.

Instead, the word *adversary* in adversarial machine learning refers to its original meaning in Latin, *adversus*, which literally means someone who "turns against" established norms and conventions. When ML systems are built, designers make certain assumptions about the place and manner of the system's operation. Anyone who opposes these assumptions or challenges the norms upon which the ML model is built is, by definition, an adversary.

Take, for example, the event held by Algorithmic Justice League, a digital advocacy nonprofit founded by Joy Buolamwini. The nonprofit holds a "Drag vs. AI" workshop where participants can paint their faces in drag makeup to fool a facial recognition system. When facial recognition systems are built, they are trained on plain, "regular" makeup faces. But if you wear over-the-top, exaggerated makeup and the facial recognition system misrecognizes you, you have turned against the established norm and are its adversary.

Text-based systems are equally fallible. It was not uncommon in the early days of AI-based résumé screening for job seekers to pad their résumé with keywords relevant to the job, colloquially called *keyword stuffing*. The rationale was that automated resume screeners were specifically looking for certain skills and keywords. The prevailing wisdom of keyword stuffers was to add the keywords on the résumé in white font, invisible to human screeners but picked up by keyword scanners to tilt the system in their favor. So, if an ML system is more likely to hire an Ivy League grad, you would simply put "Harvard" in white font in the margin, and the system would waive you through. Going against the established norm in this way made you the adversary. However, this no longer works because job sites have gotten wiser, and many now convert PDF or Word résumés to plain text, stripping all the colors and stylings.

It is not just adding words; removing or even misspelling words make a difference as well. When misinformation spreaders found that the word *ivermectin* triggered Facebook's content moderation system, they resorted to simply "ivm" or using alternate phrases like "Moo juice" and "horse paste."

Sometimes, an adversary can collectively refer to more than one person. In 2016, Microsoft released Tay, a Twitter bot that was supposed to emulate the personality of a teenager on Twitter. You could essentially tweet at Tay and have a conversation with the bot. The ML system would take your tweet as input to the ML system, process it, and respond. The key was that Microsoft Tay learned from the tweets it received to continually improve its conversational ability.

And this is where things began to go south. Tay went from a sweet 16-year-old personality to a Hitler-loving, misogynistic, bigoted bot (see Figure 1-1).

Figure 1.1　Trolls from Reddit and 4Chan poisoned the training data used in Microsoft's Twitter bot, Tay, and subsequently converted it to a bigoted bot. Geraldmellor / Twitter, Inc.

Trolls from Reddit and 4Chan descended on Twitter, intending to corrupt Tay. Why? For fun, of course! They quickly discovered that Tay was latching onto the input data and was using it to improve itself. So, the trolls flooded Tay with racist tweets. Tay picked up on this and was automatically retrained to mirror the Internet trolls. Things got so bad Microsoft decommissioned Tay within 16 hours of launching it.

Microsoft had a plan when the AI system faced individual corrupted conversations but was blindsided by this coordinated attack. This would make the group of Internet strangers the adversary. This kind of coordinated attack to corrupt the AI system's input data is called a *poisoning attack*. Just like how you can poison a village by poisoning its water source, poisoning attacks corrupt the AI system from functioning by poisoning the input data.

Then in 2022, Meta, Facebook's parent company, released an experimental chatbot called BlenderBot 3. According to the company's blog, BlenderBot 3 was "capable of searching the Internet to chat about virtually any topic. . .through natural conversations and feedback from people." Before too long, users found that the bot began parroting election conspiracies that Trump was still president "and will always be" after losing the election. It became overtly antisemitic, saying that a Jewish cabal controlling the economy was "not implausible" and that they were "over-represented among America's super-rich."

Validation of the NSCAI's warning—that attacks are happening and impacting commercial ML systems—requires at least two things: that the odds of these intentional failures are high and that motivated adversaries are willing (according to their cost-benefit calculus) to exploit them. Both of these conditions are true.

Never Tell Me the Odds

When the NSCAI report dropped, Jane Pinelis was vindicated.

Pinelis had been leading the DoD's division responsible for testing AI systems for failures and knew intimately how brittle these systems were. She had been trying to convince the Pentagon to take up the issue of defending AI systems more seriously.

So, when a bipartisan group of experts sounded the alarm about the dire straits of AI and its implications for national security, the issue gained center attention. But more importantly, the NSCAI report convinced Congress to allocate money so that experts like Pinelis were better resourced to tackle this area. In 2021, Congress authorized $740.5 million for a vast number of national defense spending programs to modernize the U.S. military. One key element of that initiative focused on trustworthy AI. Today, Pinelis is the chief of AI Assurance at the U.S. Department of Defense, where her work revolves around justified confidence in AI systems that work as intended, even in the presence of an adversary.

Pinelis prefers *justified confidence* instead of *trustworthiness* because trust is difficult to measure. Confidence, on the other hand, is a more mathematically tractable concept. Sports forecasters can provide the odds of a football team winning the Superbowl. A meteorologist can tell you the odds of it raining tomorrow.

So, what are the chances of an attacker succeeding in an attack on an ML system?

For this, we turned to David Evans, who is a professor at the University of Virginia specializing in computer security. Evans has an uncanny ability to find computer vulnerabilities and a storied expertise in this area. He never considered the possibility of hacking AI systems until one of his graduate students began experiments that systematically evaded them. When he started looking into attacking AI systems, what struck him was the lax security of current AI systems.

When you use encrypted forms of communication—say, when you send a Facebook message in Messenger or use modern-day online banking—it is built upon methods designed to provide strong encryption. These encryption schemes would be considered totally broken if there were any way to guess the secret key more efficiently than by just trying every possible combination of keys. How hard is that? you ask. The odds of compromising modern-day encryption by brute force is 1 in 10 followed by 39 zeros. In other words, the odds of an attacker breaking a modern encryption scheme just by guessing is just as likely as every air molecule in your bedroom moving to a corner, leaving you to suffocate. If a more efficient method were discovered, the encryption scheme would be considered broken and unusable for any system. These are very high-security expectations, indeed!

When designing an operating system that powers everything from your laptop to your phone, Evans pointed out that for security protection to be considered acceptable, the odds of an attack succeeding against it should be less than 1 in 400 million. That's five times rarer than the chances of you being canonized as a saint.

In both scenarios, confidence in the security of these systems comes from a combination of analyses by experts, careful testing, and the underlying fundamentals of mathematics. While it may seem that everything in IT is insecure, in reality, modern computers are more secure than ever. Believe it or not, this is the golden age of computer security.

But we are currently in the Stone Age when it comes to the security of ML models. In other words, it is comically trivial to attack AI systems—they are so bad that they routinely fail without an attacker even trying to break them! (See Table 1-2.) We already saw how Internet trolls could do it.

Table 1.2   Odds of Breaking ML Systems

	Odds of succeeding at breaking the system
Modern-day cryptography	1 in 1,000,000,000,000,000,000,000,000,000,000, 000,000,000 (1 in a duodecillion)
System security	1 in 400,000,000 (1 in 400 million)
Modern machine learning	1 in 2

Modern ML systems are so fragile that even systems built using today's state-of-the-art techniques to make them robust can *still* be broken by an adversary with little effort, succeeding in roughly half of all attempted attacks. Is our tolerance for AI robustness really 200 million times less than the tolerance for operating system robustness? Indeed, today's machine learning systems are not built with the same security reliability as your operating system or encrypted WhatsApp or Facebook messages. Should an attacker choose, most AI systems are sitting ducks.

The operating keywords here are "should an attacker choose." Who is the wizard behind the screen? Who is motivated to bring down AI systems?

AI's Achilles' Heel

In his confirmation hearings for Secretary of Defense, retired U.S. Army General Lloyd Austin called China a "pacing threat," adding that China "presents the most significant threat going forward because China is ascending."

There is no greater threat to the United States' status as the world's leader in AI than China. The NSCAI report is clear on that. That is what the NSCAI leadership reiterated to President Trump, then to everyone in the Biden administration who would listen: from Secretary of Defense General Lloyd Austin, and Deputy Secretary of Defense Kathleen Hicks to the Office of National Intelligence. At every turn, they delivered a consistent and cogent message on the urgency of seizing the moment before China's AI ascension.

For one thing, whatever the United States does, China is close at its heels. After the 2016 Cyber Grand Challenge by the U.S. government, China paid attention and held seven such competitions. When the United States announced an AI system to help fighter pilots, China announced a similar system in less than a year. When we organized a competition to help defenders get experience with attacks against AI systems, Chinese online marketplace company Alibaba took it to the next level, holding an entire series of challenges. Winners were awarded everything including T-shirts, eye massagers, handsome certificates, and a red-carpet interview process at Alibaba. Organizers also increased the prize purse over ours by 10 times for podium finishers. For those who could publish their work in a peer-reviewed, international academic journal, an additional 10,000 Chinese Yuan RMB (about $1,500 USD) was conferred.

China seems to be acutely aware of how to attack the AI systems used by the U.S. military. In a handbook used by the Chinese army, the United States' AI systems were specifically called out as susceptible to information manipulation and data poisoning. Ryan Fedasiuk, former research analyst at Georgetown University's Center for Security and Emerging Technology (CSET), noted that the Chinese handout called the issue of data in AI systems "the Achilles' heel" of the ML systems used by the U.S. Army. It gets more graphic—saying that the Chinese army can cut off, manipulate, or even overwhelm the "nerves" of U.S. AI systems with data deception, manipulation, and exhaustion. This is not a theoretical hunch. The Army Engineering University of the Chinese People's Liberation Army has participated in the AI Security challenge to upskill attacks on ML systems.

China is also pointing out another reality. "Achilles' heel" also refers to a poorly fortified target. The Chinese government routinely uses social media—namely, Facebook and Twitter—to bolster its authoritarian agenda by creating fake accounts and flooding these platforms with counter-narratives, sometimes with the same verbatim message. Unsurprisingly, social media giants have started to use AI to detect these spam accounts and shut them down. *The New York Times* and *ProPublica* reported that more than 300 Chinese-backed bot accounts posted a video attacking then Secretary of State Mike Pompeo's stance supporting the Uyghurs on Twitter. This is how three Twitter bots captioned the videos:

- *Twitter account 1*: The videos Pompeo most interested in (%
- *Twitter account 2*: The videos Pompeo most interested in ') (
- *Twitter account 3*: The videos Pompeo most interested in ^ ¥ _

Do you notice something weird at the end of each tweet? Those random characters were appended to fool Twitter's spam algorithm into thinking these tweets were distinct messages, thereby evading the AI system. Such simple tricks even confuse AI systems at mature and well-provisioned companies.

There is a corollary to China's framing of an AI Achilles' heel. Andrew Lohn, senior fellow at Georgetown University's CSET, put it succinctly when he pointed out how the ability to hack AI systems "could provide another valuable arrow in the U.S. national security community's quiver." This could deter authoritarian regimes from developing or deploying AI systems. The United States has still not fully extended deterrence into the cyber domain. However, if it moves quickly, it can use adversarial machine learning as an important arrow in that quiver to render any potential gain from AI systems from authoritarian regimes null. This seems to be unfolding already. One interesting hypothesis from Lohn is that the Russia has not fielded AI-powered weapons in the war in Ukraine because it understood the fragility of its AI-powered weapons and how these AI systems are prone to adversarial manipulation.

The Cybersecurity and Infrastructure Security Agency (CISA) within the Department of Homeland Security was founded in 2018, and has become the de facto governmental organization handling cyber threats. CISA has warned that we must have our "shield's up" for the foreseeable future to protect us from adversaries. But CISA and other government efforts are still in their infancy and have yet to find their stride for providing tactical guidance for organizations to specifically secure AI systems used in critical infrastructures.

Government agencies are not the only ones vulnerable to attacks on ML systems. As we will see, companies are unaware of ML systems attacks—as are most searchers and developers building AI systems. Scientists who studied efforts to build AI tools used in COVID diagnosis noted in their findings that, "To create models quickly, researchers frequently have relaxed standards for developing safe, reliable, and validated algorithms."

The Chinese setup of this Achilles' heel is spot on for another reason: thanks to scholars like Buolamwini who found the non-profit that organized "Drag Vs AI" workshop, Timnit Gebru, and Deborah Raji, we are increasingly aware of how AI systems can lead to biased or unfair decisions that are especially harmful to marginalized populations. However, because securing AI systems has yet to enter public discourse, the issue of attacking AI systems is virtually sub rosa in our collective conversations. Most organizations we have spoken to know how ML systems fail because of bias, but they are unaware that these systems might fail because of an active adversary. So, when an attacker compromises an AI system, it will be truly surprising, just as Achilles was culled because of a vulnerability unknown to him.

The totality of AI Achilles' heel framing—especially from what a country that the United States considers "the most significant threat going forward"—limns NSCAI into context: why it was born out of the Armed Services wing of the U.S. House of Representatives; why there was an impending urgency to get the commission's findings out; and why other democratic governments like the UK, Canada, and the EU have begun girding their loins and taking proactive measures to safeguard their AI systems.

In its final report submitted to President Trump and the U.S. Congress, the NSCAI put forth a strongly worded recommendations. The commission noted with frankness, "With rare exceptions, the idea of protecting AI systems has been an afterthought in engineering and fielding AI systems". It recommended that "at a minimum," seven organizations pay attention, including the Department of Homeland Security, Department of Defense, FBI, and State Department.

It was as if the NSCAI was awakening these high-stakes organizations to the plausible threat of attack on their AI systems. In an enigmatic voice, fit from the oracles of Delphi, the NSCAI report directed critical agencies to "Follow and incorporate advances in intentional and unintentional ML failures."

How did the NSCAI justify this recommendation? By pointing to the work of Evtimov, holding a stickered stop sign at Magnusson Park.

Chapter 2
Salt, Tape, and Split-Second Phantoms

The cartoon movie *The Mitchells vs. the Machines* is available in the kids' section of Netflix, but its representation of AI systems is quite realistic and worthy of adult attention.

The setting: the Mitchell family will have to break into the evil robot's lair to save the world. But the path ahead is perilous, peppered with highly intelligent AI robots that could spot our swashbuckling heroes.

So, the Mitchells do something unusual. They strap their derpy-looking pug, Monchi, to the front of their car and proceed to the robotic sentinels. The AI killer bots see Monchi and become utterly confused. Is this zany-looking creature a dog? A pig, perhaps? Or maybe a loaf of bread? The AI bots are soon overloaded with confusion and simply break down. The Mitchells cruise by uninhibited.

This plebian approach of causing AI systems to fail by using an unexpected object—like strapping a dog in front of the car and asking the system to reason about it—differs in sophistication from Evtimov's carefully placed stickers on the stop sign.

The stop sign attack caught the tech world's attention for its supposedly straightforward narrative: slap stickers on a stop sign, and you will confuse self-driving cars to misrecognize the signage as a speed limit. So, instead of the car coming to a halt, it would simply zip by.

But the simple-sounding punchline has a catch. The stickers were specially designed and precisely placed. The stop sign work was the brainchild of Kevin Eykholt when he was a PhD student at the University of Michigan. Eykholt pitched this idea, which ended up as a collaboration between four other universities, including the University of Washington, where Evtimov, at the time, was a PhD student himself. So, when Evtimov was holding the stop sign with the specific stickers in Magnuson Park, it was developed in collaboration with a cadre of other highbrow computer scientists, PhDs, and professors. They all used a combination of math and programming to identify the specific pattern of stickers to fool the cars' AI system responsible for identifying objects. (You can flip to the color insert to see the stop sign with the stickers.)

In the fictitious Mitchells family adventure, the pug was not altered in any way. No stickers. No modifications. No PhDs. Just the mere sight of the dog caused the cartoon AI villains to fail.

But the cartoon isn't far from reality. Let's explore how the Goliath of AI systems can be brought down—not just by the skilled Davids but also by amateurs, ragtags, and bobtails.

Challenge Accepted

It was called "the data that transformed AI research and possibly the world." But in the beginning, it was an ordinary poster hanging in the backroom of an academic convention in Miami, not too different from what you would expect in a middle school science competition.

The bulk of current ML advancements can be traced to that poster that featured the ImageNet dataset: a massive collection of labeled images compiled by Professor Fei-Fei Li and her team at Stanford. Before ImageNet, a large dataset may have consisted of 10,000 images, but Li and her team painstakingly built a dataset of more than 15 million images, each labeled and tagged with remarkable detail.

This dataset matters because one of the best (and certainly easiest) ways to get an AI system to perform better at its task is to provide it with more data. That's because of conventional wisdom that a dumb AI system with lots of data will always beat a clever one with little data. It all comes down to the scale, diversity, and quality of data.

And ImageNet was a landmark contribution, not because it was the first dataset but because it was the first truly *large-scale* dataset—1,000 times larger than the previous ones.

While Li's team certainly had quantity in their corner, ImageNet's images were also of sufficient quality to capture a scene as humans might see it. Li's team scoured the Internet, querying search engines and crawling photo-hosting sites like Flickr to find tightly focused and well-lit images that weren't too busy or noisy. The team then used humans to annotate what was in the picture. The result was a robust, full-resolution, labelled dataset that was now ready for use by researchers to train their computer vision algorithm.

With this dataset in place, Li and her team formulated the ImageNet Large Scale Visual Recognition Challenge (ILSVRC), an annual competition to track progress in computer vision. Winning the ImageNet competition, at the time, was the equivalent of winning the Olympics for ML researchers. Winners went on to receive everything from coverage in *The New York Times* to senior positions at Microsoft, Google, Baidu, and Huawei.

And, of course, there was the ensuing money. DNNResearch, the company founded by researchers who won the 2012 competition, was scooped up by Google after a secret auction in Tahoe for $44 million. Clarifai, which the 2013 winners started, raised a cool $30 million and opened offices in New York, Washington DC, and San Francisco, within three years of the event. Matching a winning entry's performance in that year was seen as a mark of quality. For instance, when Metamind's initial $8 million funding was released in 2014, the company's PR release specifically noted that it did just as well as the 2014 entry. A few years later, Metamind was acquired by Salesforce for $33 million.

The competition was popular because it helped highlight the rapid progress in computer vision. In fact, in the waning years of

ILSVRC, computer vision models surpassed average human recognition error rates on the Imagenet dataset. In some ways, it appeared that computer vision had caught up to human vision. But computer vision is also markedly different than human vision. Human vision and cognition fail when faced with distinguishing objects with nuanced differences, such as identifying a Norwich terrier from a Norfolk terrier, or distinguishing different types of Tartan fabric patterns. But for the computer vision models that won ILSVRC, identifying these nuances was a cinch.

But computers didn't always have the upper hand.

In the early years of the annual ImageNet competition, human vision still reigned supreme. Humans, on average, can identify images in the ImageNet competition dataset with about a 5 percent error rate. When the competition launched in 2010, the winning AI system had an error rate of 28 percent—far from that of human perception. Computers struggled to distinguish between shapes and details of objects that humans could intuitively identify. As the competition progressed, the error rates seemed to hover around 20 percent, and it seemed as though researchers had hit AI's capability ceiling.

However, in 2012, three researchers from the University of Toronto entered the competition and changed the game entirely—in every sense of the word. The University of Toronto group used convolutional neural networks (commonly abbreviated to CNNs), which go back to 1989 and are based on the concept of visual acuity. Acuity refers to our eyes' ability to discern or differentiate between shapes and details of objects. CNNs approximate our eyes' acuity by introducing several computational layers whose processing—after "training" the model—empirically focuses on increasingly more complex representations of the object in a sort of hierarchical fashion. For instance, in an image recognition task, the first layer of the CNN learns to identify the edges of the image—it is primarily sensitive to the orientation and thickness of line segments. In turn, the second layer tends to be sensitive to contours in the image, having connected the bits of edges from the previous layer. The third and subsequent layers gradually learn to identify prominent shapes in the image. The final "output" layer puts together the edges, contours, and shapes from the previous layers to recognize the entire image. Thus, rather than determining the image in one sweeping glance, the algorithm runs through a layer-by-layer progression of shapes and characteristics to zero in on the correct identity. With each passing year, the machine learning systems employing neural nets made fewer and fewer errors as the number of layers increased, as shown in Table 2-1.

Table 2-1   Error Rates by Network Size

ImageNet Competition Year	Size of Network	Error Rate
2010 (competition begins)	1 layer	28.2 percent
2011	1 layer	25.8 percent
2012	8 layers	16.4 percent
2013	8 layers	11.7 percent
2014	22 layers	6.7 percent
2015	152 layers	3.57 percent (beat human error of 5 percent)

The prevailing intuition: more layers imply better resolution of recognizing images and thus are better at the task at hand.

So, in 2012, University of Toronto researchers tapped into this intuition with a singular task of adding more layers to CNNs.

But the additional layers come at a cost. First, each extra layer requires more data to train the enlarged model, and second, researchers need more computing power to process the extra data. Thankfully, ImageNet provided a solution to the first requirement: more data for deep neural networks. The ImageNet database of 15 million labeled images was the perfect remedy for this ailment.

But the second issue—the increased computational burden—presented an impossible computation scenario given the commonly used computer technology of the day. So, the University of Toronto researchers tore a page from an unlikely playbook—computer gaming.

As computer gaming became popular, demand surged for realistic gameplay through graphics processing units (GPUs). While the CPU in your laptop has about 8 processing cores, GPUs typically have 100 such cores. Furthermore, while a CPU is sort of a computing generalist, each GPU core is a purpose-built number-crunching specialist especially well-suited to the kind of math employed in graphics rendering, and, as it turns out, neural networks. Having specialized cores, and many more of them means faster computation and more parallel processing ability. The Toronto researchers showed that they could leverage the power of GPUs to train neural networks. In this case, the research team built eight hidden layers into their system. Just as the 1989 paper that first introduced the concept of CNN that had lovingly come to be known as LeCun Net after its author Yann LeCun, the researchers' 2012 submission came to be known as AlexNet, after Alex Krizhevsky, the lead researcher from the University of Toronto.

With the GPU trick and the availability of more labeled data, subsequent researchers began adding more and more layers to their architecture. Thus, *deep learning* was born—the *deep* in *deep learning* and *deep neural networks* simply denotes a neural network system with many layers. With each passing year, the machine learning systems employing neural nets made fewer and fewer errors as the number of layers increased. In 2015, Microsoft released its ResNet system with a whopping 152 layers—an 18 times increase in the depth of CNN in just 2 years—which, for the first time, broke the 5 percent error human error barrier.

Ultimately, errors in ImageNet became so low that when the last version of the competition was held in 2017, the winning entry had an error rate of 2 percent—less than half of what humans could do on the same dataset. Many in the research community consider ImageNet to be "solved," and any algorithm that has a lower than 5 percent error in ImageNet challenge has been called *superhuman.*

It turns out, however, that AI systems are not superhuman. In the right circumstances, they are not really even super.

When Expectation Meets Reality

Without overthinking, what do you see in the images in Figure 2-1? If you guessed a bird, a painting, and a butterfly, then congratulations! You are 100 percent human!

Figure 2-1   What's in these pictures? Courtesy of Dan Hendrycks

According to the winning algorithm from the 2015 ImageNet competition, these images represent a jeep, goldfish, and washing machine. (You can see the color images in the color insert.)

The images are part of a dataset that researcher Dan Hendrycks and others curated to demonstrate the limitations of the current state of computer vision. They assembled a selection of naturally confounding images to show that you don't need an attacker in a hoodie to trick a state-of-the-art machine; Mother Nature is sometimes good enough. The error rate rocketed to 98 percent when Hendrycks' team tested several ImageNet-winning algorithm architectures that could classify with astonishing accuracy on their confounding dataset.

How was this possible? If you squint your eye and look at the butterfly under the table, it might remind you—very tangentially—of a washing machine's lint screen. Maybe that's what is also confusing the ML system. But, since ML systems do not explain their reasoning, your guess is as good as ours.

Humans learn to identify objects in scenes that are decomposable. For example, we can identify fish in multiple contexts: in a painting, on a plate, or in a pond. While we may take cues from the background, we are not beholden to those cues. For instance, if you were to see a fish in an absurd setting—on the living room sofa—you would still be able to recognize it as a fish.

But machines do not have this same power of decomposition and reasoning about objects. A Twitter account with the @ResNext-Guesser (it is a play on Microsoft's ImageNet winning AI system, ResNet) handle allows you to inspect this phenomenon. Users can post pictures and memes to @ResNextGuesser and discover how AI systems identify them. For instance, a picture of a tower of yellow cheese slices is confidently identified as pineapple. A refrigerator filled with eggs is classified as ping-pong balls with 99 percent confidence. In another homage to *The Mitchells vs. the Machines*, it misidentified a chihuahua dog as a muffin.

Machine learning's raison d'être is to predict about data it has never seen before. All the accuracy numbers we have seen from the ImageNet competition are from practice tests in ideal conditions. ImageNet data is pristine, patiently labeled, and high quality. But in real-world exams, our algorithms flounder because data can be unexpected. For instance, if an AI system was trained on pictures of butterflies perched on flowers, then showing an image of a butterfly perched on a dog or table—or even a different type of flower than used in training—would break the AI system. As we will see, the AI system is not really generalizing the concept of identifying objects in any setting. Generalization for the AI system means doing well beyond one dataset. It means doing well in the real world.

Nowhere is the gulf between testing ML algorithms in controlled situations and in real-world testing wider than with autonomous vehicles.

MIT's self-driving car spinoff, nuTonomy, was acquired for $450 million just 4 years after the company was launched, and it had the receipts to show it was worth the price. nuTonomy had inked deals with Lyft, Grab, Peugeot, and autonomous driving pilots in Singapore. As it piloted in tropical, sunny Singapore, nuTonomy also was engaged in phased piloting on its home turf of Boston.

In February 2017, nuTonomy received approval from the City of Boston to expand the testing of its autonomous vehicles. However, February weather in Beantown comes with a lot of snow. The falling snow altered how the sensors perceived the car's surroundings, causing problems for the vehicle. It turns out that this is not just a sensor issue; it is a lack of data issue. There aren't many datasets of cars driving in snowy conditions because much of the autonomous vehicle testing is done in warmer parts of California, Texas, Arizona, and Florida.

Autonomous vehicle testing wasn't just affected by inclement weather. Sometimes, the banalest objects encountered while driving, like the pug in the *Mitchells* movie, confounded autonomous vehicles. For instance, according to a report prepared by the World Economic Forum, seagulls posed a problem for nuTonomy. The cars came to a standstill every time seagulls stood on the road. nuTonomy's sensors identified an object on the road and refused to move until cleared. (Later, the engineers made the vehicle slowly inch forward to shoo away the seagulls.)

This is not a problem endemic to one car manufacturer. The Insurance Institute for Highway Safety (IIHS), a U.S. nonprofit that curates commercial vehicle safety ratings, reached a similar conclusion in 2018 when it tested adaptive cruise control in various cars. For instance, they found that Tesla's Model 3 slowed down seven times in their testing when it encountered shadows of trees.

Bridges are another problem for most self-driving cars. When Uber was testing its autonomous cars in Pittsburgh, it found that bridges were hard for its systems to negotiate. This is a bit of a problem because Pittsburgh—the City of Bridges—has 446 of them.

Such failures are now so commonplace you can find many such videos on YouTube. For instance, Tesla's AI system misrecognized a rising full moon as a traffic signal, with the moon glow perhaps being interpreted as the yellow light of a traffic semaphore. In another case, Tesla users reported that cars slowed down in front of the Burger King billboards displaying the fast-food restaurant's circular logo with its name written in red between two yellow buns.

Perhaps Tesla's AI system also misrecognized these to be signals to yield? One can only surmise.

Burger King was the clear winner here. It capitalized on this gaffe with its #autopilotwhopper ad campaign, giving smart car drivers a free burger when visiting their restaurants.

The good news is that AI systems in autonomous vehicles are always improving, given the rapid progress in AI as a field and the ability to update these systems constantly. For instance, Tesla was able to remediate the Burger King problem via a software update.

However, self-driving cars are not the only ones suffering from this malady. In response to school shootings, some schools across the United States have deployed scanners that use AI to detect guns in backpacks. An investigation by *Vice* showed a litany of everyday items these AI scanners mistake for guns: water bottles, eyeglass cases, umbrellas, certain kinds of three-ring binders, Chromebooks, and laptops. In the same way that models trained on ImageNet bewilderingly mistook a butterfly for a washing machine, to the schools' computers vision systems, these ordinary objects all seemed very gun-like.

But the consequence here is more serious. In one of the schools with the AI gun detector, many false alarms were sounded on the day the scanner was deployed. The school's principal wrote, "Today was probably the least safe day" because resources were re-routed to do manual searches on the kids. The worst part of the entire AI gun detector fiasco? In some cases, the AI scanner failed to detect the one thing they were supposed to detect: guns.

The takeaway here is that AI systems operate on a fundamental assumption that the data they are tested on is similar to the data they are trained on. When that assertion fails, the performance of the AI system becomes unreliable. But does this mean that if we test the system using images that are almost exactly what it was trained on, the AI systems are guaranteed to work? It depends.

Color Me Blind

When you look at Figure 2-2, you probably do not see a king penguin, a green snake, and a school bus. If you did, that would make you a state-of-the-art ML model trained on ImageNet. (For this one, you may want to flip to this book's centerfold to see the pictures in color.)

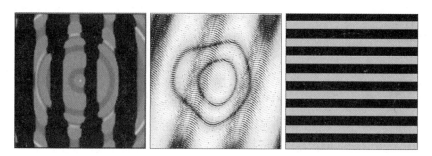

Figure 2-2   What do you see in these pictures? Courtesy of Anh Nguyen

While the three pictures in Figure 2-1 were unaltered images with no additional sleight of hand, the pictures in Figure 2-2 were specifically constructed to confuse AI systems. The striking thing is that a particular model that otherwise performs quite well on ImageNet or even in broader image classification is very convinced—99.92 percent confident, to be precise—that the rings in the first picture represent a penguin.

This is because AI systems latch on to the images' color, shape, and texture during the training phase and use this spurious correlation to identify images.

We can see this intuitively. For instance, the image with black vertical bars with gray concentric circles was classified as a penguin, perhaps because penguins tend to have black and gray overcoats.

When we remove colors or tinker with the image's texture, AI systems tend to be confused. For instance, researchers trained neural networks on regular images and tested them on photos of glass figurines. Glass figurines do not have the color or texture information encoded in regular images, so it is much more difficult to classify them, and state-of-the-art AI systems floundered when faced with this task. Researchers trained AI systems on regular, colored images but tested them on glass figurines without color or texture cues. They found that AI systems fared poorly in identifying glass figurines. For instance, the schooner shown in Figure 2-3 was identified as a can opener.

Figure 2-3   An AI system misidentified this model of a schooner as a can opener. Courtesy of Nicholas Baker

AI systems' overreliance on color and shape has real-world implications. A small gardening business in Canada posted on Facebook about its Walla Walla onions, describing them as "sweet, mild, and large" and easy to grow from seed (see Figure 2-4). Facebook's algorithms mistakenly flagged this post as sexually suggestive, only to later acknowledge the gaffe and reinstate the post. Facebook Canada's head of communications told CBC News that Facebook uses automation to identify nudity, but "sometimes it doesn't know a Walla Walla onion from a, well, you know." It's easy to dismiss this as a gaffe, but flagged accounts have serious consequences for small businesses. They can lose thousands of dollars by being deprioritized in feeds or banned. Even when reinstated, it takes time for the algorithm to begin promoting the account's content again.

Like Facebook, blogging platform Tumblr used AI to detect pornographic content, and like Facebook, the AI system made errors (see Figure 2-4). In 2018, Tumblr also faced a similar problem when it decided not to continue hosting adult content on its platform. Confused Tumblr users took to Twitter with the #toosexyfortumblr hashtag to show how their seemingly prosaic images were flagged.

Figure 2-4   Tumblr's AI-based porn detection system triggered on banal content like this doll, perhaps because it is phallic shaped with skin color.
Ruemxu / Twitter, Inc.

From images of Jesus Christ in a loincloth to superheroes in spandex to cartoons using skin color, the "puritanical" AI system took no prisoners and censored them all. Even an iconic picture of Mister Rogers and Officer Clemons dipping their legs in the pool was flagged. Too much ankle? A similar AI system used by the London Metropolitan Police Department to identify child pornography kept incorrectly flagging pictures of desert wallpaper because it resembled skin color.

Sometimes, like the AI weapon scanners that failed to detect the actual guns, content moderation algorithms fail to catch actual child pornography. Through an investigation from the *Verge* publication, Twitter's own employees concluded that "Twitter cannot accurately detect child sexual exploitation and non-consensual nudity at scale" and found that the tool used for such detection was "most fragile, inefficient, and under-supported."

AI systems identifying problematic content at scale can help human reviewers prioritize tricky content and possibly ameliorate the trauma of repeatedly seeing disturbing content. But, as we have seen, AI systems are error-prone because of their idiosyncrasies, such as latching on to color when identifying images. The very companies deploying AI systems for content moderation—Facebook, Tumblr, Instagram, and Twitter—acknowledge that their systems are error-prone and they must continually work to improve them.

In 1964, U.S. Supreme Court Justice Stewart Potter famously wrote that he couldn't describe what obscenity is, but "I know it when I see it." More than 50 years in, AI systems are mistaking onions for, well, you know.

Translation Fails

On August 4, 2017, the technology magazine *Verge* reported that "Facebook's translations were now powered completely by AI." Facebook had radically improved its translation system by employing machine learning. Each of the 4.5 billion daily Facebook Translate translations was completely powered by neural networks. Facebook's blog post announcing this transition to complete algorithmic automation ended with a sense of optimism: "We will continue to push the boundaries of neural machine translation technology, with the aim of providing humanlike translations to everyone on Facebook."

And like humans, these translations are not perfect, as one construction worker in the Palestinian Beitar settlement found out on October 4, 2017. Leaning against a bulldozer and balancing a cup of coffee and a cigarette, a smiling Palestinian man posted "Good Morning" in Arabic on Facebook. Soon enough, he was arrested by the Israeli West Bank police on "suspicion of incitement" based on his Facebook post. Why? Someone in the Israeli police force had used Facebook's translation system to translate the Arabic post to Hebrew, rendering it incorrectly as "hurt them." When the same Arabic post was translated to English, Facebook mistranslated it to "attack them." Facebook's translation system failed to reliably translate Arabic not in one but two languages. The construction worker had used the caption (يصبحهم) "yusbihuhum," which is just one character away from (يذبحهم) "yethbihuhum," or "he slaughters." This single change in character (ص to ذ) would be apparent to any native Arabic speakers based on the context and usage. However, no Arabic-speaking officers were consulted before the arrest. It was only after questioning the man for hours that the Israeli police realized it was a mistake and released him.

A similar incident occurred in 2018 with Google Translate. A police officer in the United States pulled over a driver who spoke Spanish but very little English. Not speaking Spanish and wanting to search the car, the officer turned to Google Translate to render his English question in Spanish. "¿Puedo buscar el auto?" the officer parroted to the driver from Google Translate. The perhaps confused driver responded affirmatively. Spanish speakers would immediately spot the gaffe. Google Translate provided the Spanish equivalent of "Can I identify the car?" as in spot the car. The right word, instead of *buscar*, would be *registrar*, which denotes searching. A judge later ruled that this was a warrantless search because Google's translation was so off-base that the driver could not have comprehended it. The judge wrote that "Google Translate provides literal but nonsensical translation" and "it is not reasonable for an officer to use and rely on Google Translate to obtain consent."

The solution to these sorts of failures is seen as a lack of context. The translation systems are not provided with the surrounding information to provide the correct information. But even when the context is provided, things can go awry.

WeChat, the Chinese super app used by a billion people around the world, translated the neutral Chinese phrase "hei laowai"—meaning "black foreigner"—as the highly prejudicial and offensive n-word. However, WeChat seemed to do this only when "hei laowai" was used in a negative context, such as being tardy or being a thief. When the Chinese phrase was used in a neutral or positive setting, such as a birthday wish, WeChat's machine learning system used the correct translation. The ML model presumably had learned the racist translations from actual racist utterances used with negative connotations in training data.

While Facebook and WeChat eventually apologized for each of their mistranslations, these incidents show that algorithmic interpretations can be fraught with difficulties. We place enormous trust in these fragile systems, even in high-stakes outcomes. Using ML-powered translation to translate a restaurant menu is one thing, but employing it without human review in law enforcement is a totally different ball game.

Attacking AI Systems via Fails

"David and Goliath (/ˌdeɪvəd ən ɡəˈlaɪəθ/): used for describing a situation in which a small person or organization defeats a much larger one in a surprising way." —Macmillan Dictionary

Everybody loves this underdog story: the large, overrated Goliath is unexpectedly brought down by the small David. One of the big downfalls of today's largely overrated AI systems is that they fail to account for the amateur attackers, the underdog usurpers.

The fact of the matter is that all modern AI systems will produce at least some erratic behavior under the right conditions. This has ramifications when one considers the presence of a motivated adversary—sophisticated or not—that is somehow incentivized to exploit the erratic behavior.

It might be tempting to brush off the low-skilled attacks, but that is Goliath-style thinking. Low-skilled does not mean low impact. We will see how ML-controlled navigation systems are confused with things you are likely to find in your home—from table salt to your movie projector. AI systems don't "learn." Instead, they can recognize systems by latching onto arbitrary characteristics of the image or text. When an adversary alters these significant characteristics, they can mislead AI systems.

Is this adversarial machine learning? Indeed, these are adversaries in the sense that they present worst-case inputs to an AI system. They do it for entertainment, to make a statement, or for monetary gain. However, that the adversaries are subverting an AI system might be wholly irrelevant to them. What these attacks lack in mathematical sophistication, they make up for in cleverness. The bottom line is that one need not be a math whiz to attack an AI system.

For a limited time, if you had searched for "bad writers" in Google's search engine, the first picture would have been the *Game of Thrones* creators (see Figure 2-5). You can thank Reddit users who were severely disappointed by the final season of HBO's television adaptation of George R.R. Martin's *Song of Ice and Fire* book series. True to its "front page of the Internet" tagline, Reddit users post content that may be upvoted by other users. One Reddit user started a discussion thread entitled "Bad Writers. Upvote this post so it's the first result when you google 'Bad Writers'" and included a photo of the show's writers, David Benioff and D.B. Weiss. The post gained popularity—more than 51,000 users upvoted it. Since Reddit is a Top 20 globally visited site, it contributed heavily to Google's search algorithm's (momentary) decision to index the picture with the keywords "bad writers."

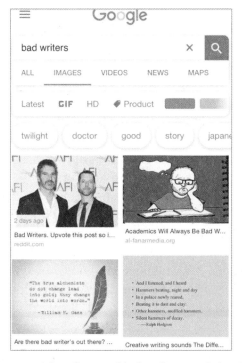

Figure 2-5   Disappointed fans from Reddit briefly "Google bombed" Google's search engine to associate "bad writers" with an image of the Game of Thrones TV show writers.
SOURCE: Reddit/bmcc9n

Tricking search engines to surface irrelevant content at the top of the search results is colloquially called *Google bombing* but extends to all search engines.

Bing, Microsoft's search engine, launched a new feature to make finding popular and trending videos easier by highlighting them at the top of the search page. In July 2020, Ars Technica found that when users searched for the keyword "shutterstock" (the popular stock footage company), they were presented with crudely titled results that were purported to be pornographic. For instance, a video purporting to be a graphic video of a nude female was actually a bird from the Paridae family called a *tit*. The videos' descriptions were specifically altered—presumably by an internet troll—to cause them to trend on the search engine. Microsoft fixed the issue by disabling the trending feature.

Maps can also be manipulated. With its 1 billion+ users across 220 countries, Google Maps is projected to be a big cash cow for its parent company, Alphabet. When navigating using Google Maps, users get access to real-time traffic information. If there is bumper-to-bumper traffic, the entire route is shaded red, and alternate routes are presented (and, sometimes, even automatically rerouted). Using machine learning, Google Maps uses data from various sources to predict traffic information: historical traffic patterns over time, authoritative data from local governments to learn about speed limits and construction, and data from its users.

This last source—data from its users, specifically, the GPS data from users' mobile phones—is a great indicator to estimate traffic density. When a bunch of Google Maps users driving in the same area reduce their speed, this could mean slow traffic. That's when you see the dreaded red route coloring on Google Maps.

This GPS data from the users can be manipulated, which is exactly what artist Simon Weckert did. Weckert walked slowly up and down a street on a Berlin bridge (see Figure 2-6) with a red wagon filled with 99 Android phones, all running Google Maps in car mode. To Google's algorithm processing this data in the data-centers, this appeared very much like 99 cars in the street, all moving at a snail's pace. From this, Google inferred that there was a huge traffic jam. Google Maps users found that Berlin bridge was shaded in red—falsely indicating heavy traffic—and may have received recommendations from Google Maps to take alternate routes. In reality, however, the street was empty.

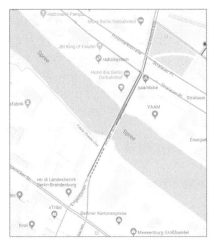 

Figure 2-6 By filling a wagon with 99 Android phones running Google Maps and walking slowly on an empty street, Google Maps was tricked into thinking there was heavy traffic.
Simon Weckert

This was not the first time Google Maps was bitten by relying on user input to its system. In 2015, members of a technology discussion board first spotted a fictitious park near the city of Rawalpindi in Pakistan on Google Maps. The shape of the park? Google's Android logo relieving itself on Apple's logo. Around that time, Google had been improving its maps by fostering a community of amateur cartographers to suggest changes and add missing landmarks. While peers generally reviewed changes before submitting, the system was set up so that highly trusted contributions were more laxly reviewed—and that was how the fictitious Pakastani park materialized for worldwide users. Soon after imposing a strict review process, the feature was disabled.

But made-up places can be insidious. In 2019, journalists from *The Wall Street Journal* searched for plumbers in New York City and found that out of the top 20 results returned by Google, 13 were fake businesses posing as plumbers. Online advertising specialists estimate that there could be 11 million fake places at any point in time on Google Maps. While hotels and restaurants are less likely to be fake, *The Wall Street Journal* found that plumbers, electricians, towing and car repair services, and law offices are more likely to have fake locations. While Google Maps attempts to verify every location, *The Wall Street Journal* reported that you could get your own fake listing by contracting shady firms. They will do it for $99. . .or $8,599 for a 100-pack.

Autonomous Trap 001

Without overthinking, what number do you see in Figure 2-7?

Figure 2-7   Simple electrical tape on speed signs confused Tesla's sensors to misrecognize the speed limit as 85.
McAfee, LLC

Well, by now, you know the game. Nothing is as it seems.

In this case, using simple tape, researchers from McAfee tested their hypothesis that simply elongating the 3 digit could confuse the MobilEye sensor used in the Tesla Model X (2016) and Tesla Model S (2016) to identify the speed limit from traffic signs. While they found that sophisticated placement of stickers, like Evtimov's stop sign attack, can trick the sensors, so did a single piece of black electrical tape. By using tape to extend the middle of the number 3, the MobilEye sensors misrecognized the posted 35 mph as 85, causing the car to accelerate. Researchers noted that when there was a discrepancy between GPS tagging and posted signs in their experiments, previous Tesla models defaulted to the posted sign, trusting its computer sight over the GPS map.

This trick stands out because, unlike the special stickers Evtimov and the PhD crew stuck on stop signs, this one is just plain old electric tape that you can find at Home Depot. Anyone can pull it off; no computer science degree required.

Failures in self-driving have become an intense area of study for two reasons: cars are easy targets to confuse because the input to their image recognition system includes sensory data of the entire surroundings. Your Alexa needs to function well only in the context of a 500-square-foot room with surroundings that don't change. Your self-driving car must reason in dynamic conditions—from snow to seagulls. Naturally, nature creates more failure modes.

Also, finding failures in self-driving cars gets attention. From newspapers to policy briefs, homage is paid to these attacks, warning us about how a simple trick can fool a complicated car. This taps into our inner David and Goliath sentiment—how a behemoth of an AI system can be confused by simple stickers. AI systems perform well most of the time, though we have already seen how banal objects like bridges and shadows can confuse them. So, what happens when a motivated adversary actively tries to bring the system down?

One way to disrupt a self-driving car is to simply draw a circle around it. James Bridle custom-built a neural network vision system and attached it to his car. To demonstrate his own computer vision system's limitation, he drew two concentric circles: the inner circle was a solid line, and the outer circle was a dashed line. When he drove his self-made, self-driving car complete with cameras and ML algorithms, he could drive into the circle but not out of it (see Figure 2-8). This is because the car confused the circles with lane markings. A dashed line is a road marking that tells drivers (human and autonomous) that it is okay to change lanes; solid lines indicate that one must not change lanes. While entering through the dashed line, the self-driving car refused to exit on the solid line, thus taking the car prisoner. (Bridle appropriately titled his work "Autonomous Trap 001.") He drew the circles using salt and called them "salt circles," a reference to the pagan rituals using salt to contain spirits.

Figure 2-8   A self-driving car is immobilized because it confuses the salt circle for lane markings.
Screen capture from Source: Autonomous Trap 001 (James Bridle, 2017), courtesy of the artist

The previous mischiefs all left a trace. Tape on the sign. Salt on the ground. What distinguishes the next attack is that it can go completely unobserved by humans. Using a movie projector, researchers from Ben-Gurion University momentarily projected a human image onto the road. The phantom image existed for a mere 125 millisecond—short enough for humans to miss it, but long enough for Tesla's sensors to pick it up. The projected image confused Tesla's computer vision system into thinking it had detected a pedestrian inconveniently walking right in front of the car. Brakes!

The researchers had fun with this one. Cheekily, they chose Elon Musk as the image to project on the road. Next, they projected stop signs on trees, confusing the car. Then, they projected lanes on the road, and the car veered. And unlike tape or table salt hacks, phantoms don't leave any evidence at the scene—an adversarial AI crime with a clean getaway.

But all is not yet doom and gloom. For the most part, you are safe in your self-driving car. Several conditions need to line up to execute such attacks. Just because the salt circle trick works on Bridle's neural network does not necessarily mean it will work on your autonomous car. The sticker work comes with these strings attached:

- The tape's color. (Black seemed to perform well; red and reflective, not so much.)
- The relative position of the tape. (A gap between the tape and the number 3 on the sign did not work well.)
- The angle at which the sensors observe the sign.

All these would have to line up for the attack to work—a tough sell.

Additionally, Tesla cars no longer use MobilEye sensors, and the system can supplement identifying speed limits by tapping into the maps of the area. Furthermore, future versions of MobilEye will supposedly ameliorate these kinds of attacks. Even though it is after the fact, we can take solace in that autonomous vehicles generally can update their software regularly, repairing buggy behavior.

What we should take away is that autonomous vehicles of all stripes need to foresee the presence of a motivated adversary and actively invest in forestalling adversarial manipulation.

Common Corruption

Researchers in 2018 found that simply changing the hue (color) and saturation (color intensity) of images dropped the accuracy of an AI system, which previously won the ImageNet challenge, from the high 90s to just 6 percent. Every time the hue and saturation changed, the same image of the bird was recognized as an airplane, dog, and frog (see Figure 2-9). (You can flip to the insert to see this image in color).

And this trick was intuitively exploited by Tumblr adversaries after the platform banned pornographic content on its website. The users discovered that by coloring the pictures green and including a picture of a cartoon owl, the filter would not recognize the image as pornographic. Because the AI system was apparently cueing on colors—like the color of the skin—to identify whether content was pornographic, it was more likely to let green bodies slip by.

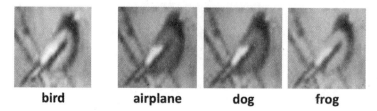

bird   **airplane**   **dog**   **frog**

Figure 2-9   Changing the hue and saturation of the image also changes how AI algorithms perceive it. (Best viewed in color.) Courtesy of Hossein Hosseini

The Mitchells vs. the Machines trick for confusing AI systems with a pug in front of the car is explained in a paper entitled, "The Elephant in the Room." Researchers from York University and the University of Toronto found that state-of-the-art AI systems failed in computer vision tasks when something unexpected appeared in an image. For instance, putting a polar bear on a sunny backyard patio confused the AI system into misrecognizing it as a car. When you place seemingly out-of-place objects—like a pug in front of the car—AI systems are more likely to misidentify them. See Figure 2-10.

Figure 2-10   The boxes show how the AI algorithm recognizes the objects. When a random polar bear is added to the picture, the AI system is confused—and a car is erroneously detected. Courtesy of Amir Rosenfeld

Even simply cropping or rotating images can confuse AI systems. MIT researchers found that rotated images can completely change the judgment made by an AI system. For instance, simply rotating the picture of a bird now makes the AI system recognize it incorrectly as an orangutan (see Figure 2-11).

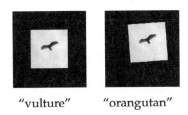

"vulture"   "orangutan"

Figure 2-11 Simply cropping and rotating the image causes the AI system to misrecognize images. Courtesy of Logan Engstrom, Brandon Tran, and Dimitris Tsipras

Why should I care? you ask.

Take AI for medicine. In 2018, Scott Gotleib, then FDA commissioner, wrote that AI "holds enormous promise for the future of medicine" when approving one of the early trials of AI in medical diagnosis. But that promise may be in peril if ML systems' brittle nature leaves them susceptible to attack.

Researchers from Harvard and MIT showed that the mere act of rotating an image of a lesion can cause the AI system to change the diagnosis—very confidently. Not only can it lead to a missed cancer diagnosis, rotating the image can also flip the diagnosis from benign to malignant (see Figure 2-12). Why would anyone do that? Insurance fraud. Imagine a dermatologist holding the camera at a weird angle to take pictures to bilk the insurance company. It brings new meaning to the phrase, "The diagnosis is in the doctor's hands."

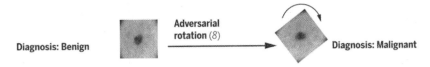

Diagnosis: Benign   Adversarial rotation (8)   Diagnosis: Malignant

Figure 2-12 All it takes to attack a state-of-the-art AI healthcare algorithm is to rotate the image. Courtesy of Samuel G. Finlayson

The core of the problem is that machine learning systems use shortcuts to learn. They latch onto backgrounds, clutch to color, turn to texture—and are simply conditioned on cues.

It is not the use of shortcuts that's problematic. Humans use shortcuts, too. We use acronyms to recall colors of the rainbow, remember a colleague by the color of their hair, and associate memories with smells. The constant oversell of AI having superhuman abilities and the barrage of headlines of AI superiority are odious. This overtrust puts us at risk—from worthless porn filters to incarceration of the innocent.

Here is the kicker: All it takes for an attacker to confuse a complicated ML algorithm is to identify and hack these shortcuts. An amateur can cause traffic jams on Google Maps with a wagon full of phones, entrap a self-driving car with salt and electric tape, and evade porn filters by coloring the pictures green.

So, if that's what an amateur can do, what damage could be caused by a skilled researcher or motivated adversary?

Chapter 3
Subtle, Specific, and Ever-Present

By any measure, the attack that fooled AI systems in autonomous vehicles into misrecognizing a stop sign for a speed limit sign by using a carefully designed arrangement of stickers was famous. It would be exhibited at the celebrated Science Museum in London alongside Boaty McBoatface, an unmanned underwater vehicle whose name was chosen by the British public. Eventually, the very stop sign used to misdirect AI systems underpinning autonomous vehicles at Magnuson Park would become part of the museum's permanent collection.

Only one other attack on AI systems has similarly gripped the imagination of the AI populace. In fact, if you read about securing AI systems—be it in news articles, policy briefs, or even highbrow academic research—you simply cannot escape its mention. It has come to iconify the entire field of adversarial machine learning, and the work that generated it has become foundational to other machine learning evasion attacks—including the stop sign sticker attack.

As you will see, the attack involves imperceptible changes to an image. For example, look at the two images in Figure 3-1 and decide which is a panda and which is a gibbon.

Figure 3.1   Panda or gibbon? Courtesy of Ian Goodfellow14

No, we are not crazy. To the human eye, both photos clearly show the same image of a panda. But the picture on the left has been altered imperceptibly, modified only slightly from the original image, but sufficient for a relatively sophisticated AI system to misrecognize it as a gibbon!

The recipe to launch this attack differs from others we have seen so far. It is *subtle*: the changes to the image are often imperceptible to humans. It is *specific*: the modifications are not arbitrary—only a careful manipulation in just the right way causes baffling behavior in the AI. To discover this worst-case modification, the attacker relies on the very tools used to train AI *to fool* it. This form of attack is also *ever-present*, affecting all known ML systems to date. No ML model is immune from this attack.

You may already see why this is consequential. The same principles that can make an AI system mistake a panda for a gibbon can be used to mistake a bus for an ostrich, a banana for a toaster, a 1 for a 9, or a stop sign for a speed limit sign. An adversary can distort the reality that machines perceive and, thus, exploit our trust in them.

The genius in this attack follows the story of science: perspicacity, parallel discoveries, persistence, and a pinch of good old luck.

Intriguing Properties of Neural Networks

A research work entitled "Intriguing Properties of Neural Networks" had all the trappings of a landmark paper when it was posted in 2014 at a famous machine learning conference called ICLR (often pronounced "eye-clear"). The primary author, Cristian Szegedy, was affiliated with Google, had already established himself as a deep learning juggernaut, and would go on to help Google win the ImageNet competition. A coauthor, Ilya Sutskever, was part of the original winning team that had already won the ImageNet competition and sparked the deep learning revolution. Between its alluring title and the cachet of its (quite literally) award-winning authors, one thing was certain: people would be paying attention to this paper.

A hitherto unknown graduate student, Ian Goodfellow, was among the list of luminary authors. When Goodfellow received an offer to intern at Google, he was elated. He was a graduate student at one of the most celebrated and well-resourced labs run by revered AI pioneer Yoshua Bengio. But being a graduate student was no match for a Google internship's unparalleled perks, including "Googley extras." Beyond the handsome salary and an opportunity to work on real-world problems where data and compute were readily available without constraints, Google showered its interns with free housing, gym memberships, transportation, and massages. And, of course, they were provided with the most famous perk of all—free food. This is not your run-of-the-mill free food. How good can it be? you are thinking. A food reviewer from *Serious Eats* magazine wrote: "Lunch at Google HQ (Head Quarters) is as Insanely Awesome as You Thought." On the day the reviewer visited one of Google's numerous cafés—each with its own theme—lunch included in-house baked bread and honey, kale salad with squash, corn dumplings, locally sourced Rockfish encrusted with nuts, and pecan bars that were described as "light and borderline savory, with just a faint touch of maple, and garbanzo flour to render these gluten-free." All this free food was focused on making employees happy and providing a setting where they could freely collaborate.

Unlike today, where Google's AI research hub spans from Accra to Zurich, Goodfellow interned when the laboratory was small enough for one to know everyone else. This was a networking boon. Like all interns, he was excited to meet the big kahunas at Google and make their connections. So, over the free food in Google's cavernous cafeteria, Goodfellow met Szegedy, who Goodfellow considered a "hotshot" and was fishing for any chance to work with him.

For some time, Szegedy had been pondering what he thought was an important problem. As he was experimenting with neural networks, he found that by slightly changing pixel colors in an image, the neural network failed to recognize the original image. He called these "funny perturbations" because they quite readily caused the system to misclassify images—which he thought was hilarious. Nothing provides more comedic relief than big systems failing.

Szegedy's spidey sense told him this was big, so he relentlessly showed these perturbed images to anyone who would listen. It looked like a bus to us, but for the state-of-the-art ML systems of the time, it was an ostrich! Most people, though, didn't pay attention. Neural networks, especially, would fail at the slightest image perturbation. People were already aware of mistakes from unintentional failures like AI systems misrecognizing onions as pornographic material. Most who saw Szegedy's "funny perturbations" suggested things would get better with time as the neural networks became bigger and learned from more data. Experts of the day gently put down his concerns.

Szegedy almost shelved the entire idea until another Google colleague, Wojciech "Woj" Zaremba, took interest.

It was at this opportune moment that Goodfellow inveigled an invitation for lunch with Szegedy. And so over free food in Google's cafeteria, Szegedy, needing an extra pair of hands to get the research through the finish line, asked what he thought was a smart intern to help him out. In his zest to impress Szegedy, Goodfellow gladly agreed and began optimizing Szegedy's initial discoveries.

But all through the internship, Goodfellow really didn't believe Szegedy's line of research was consequential. Like Szegedy's critics who turned away his ideas, Goodfellow also believed there was nothing novel or interesting about the failure of neural networks. He also thought the solution to the perturbing pixels problem confusing the classifier was trivial. "I didn't think it would be very hard to get rid of," he told us. The entire time he was working on the project, Goodfellow simply thought of it as "doing a favor" for "hotshot" Szegedy.

Beyond optimizing Szegedy's code, Goodfellow also made another contribution: changing Szegedy's name for this phenomenon from "funny perturbations" to "adversarial examples." It was rooted in game theory, where the perturbations were worst-case inputs an adversary might present to confuse a model. The new moniker also had an unplanned effect. The notion of an adversary—a malicious attacker who could topple the system—lent some gravitas to the situation. While people may dismiss "funny perturbations" as a parlor trick pablum, the rebranding ushered in some much-needed solemnity and seriousness. *What's in a name?* you ask. The moniker, adversarial examples, now defines the entire field of securing AI systems.

Even after Szegedy published the paper in 2013, Goodfellow was doubtful about the idea, but Google's free lunch would play a role again in advancing the field.

By 2014, Goodfellow had transitioned from an intern to a full-time employee at Google Brain. He was poking around with defending against adversarial examples. He quickly coded up his idea, kick-started the experiment on the computer, and went to the café for lunch. When he returned, he found that the experiment had broken all previous defense records. State-of-the-art techniques that claimed to protect against adversarial examples just crumbled. This all happened in the time it took for him to survey and sup at Google Café's saporous spread. For the first time, Goodfellow was genuinely excited about the area. He eventually published the results containing the now-famous panda-gibbon picture. After that 2014 publication, Goodfellow took the baton and ran with adversarial examples for close to six years, illuminating the world how they are subtle, specific, and ever-present.

They Are Everywhere

The mischiefs we saw in Chapter 2—rotating an image or changing its color—can already inflict pain on state-of-the-art ML systems. But if we liken the hijinks in the previous chapter to a machete, adversarial examples are scalpels.

The first thing to note is that adversarial examples are subtle. In the previous chapter, we saw how salt, stickers, or electric tape could dupe machine learning systems. That mischief is somewhat obvious if a human were to investigate why the system erred. Adversarial examples, on the other hand, have the potential to fool both humans and the machine learning system. Humans reviewing only the system's input see no aberration, so they are unlikely to detect tampering. Human oversight in critical situations—like determining if you are eligible for a loan, medical imaging, or autonomous defense—is extraordinarily important. But if only inspecting the input, adversarial examples are subtle enough to evade human oversight.

Another reason adversarial examples are potent is that discovering them is done in a specific manner that can be automated. No human is manually looking for which pixel in the panda photo must be altered to fool the image recognition system into misrecognizing it as a gibbon. The search to confuse AI systems is guided by the very tools used to train ML models themselves. In fact, if you try to alter pixels randomly, the AI system is not likely to be confused. For adversarial examples to be effective, the process needs to be smart, methodical, and algorithmic—all of which can be automated.

This algorithmically guided and automated search can yield results that convincingly fool AI systems. Adversarial AI clothing is a peculiar adversarial example. Designed to evade facial recognition systems, adversarial examples can be printed onto everyday clothing: T-shirts become adversarial T-shirts, and glasses become adversarial glasses. For instance, what looks like a sweater with a psychedelic, multicolor, swirly design is actually a carefully constructed pattern to fool object recognition systems into thinking the wearer does not exist (see Figure 3-2). Want the facial recognition system to think you are actress Milla Jovovich of *The Fifth Element* fame? Researchers from Carnegie Mellon 3D printed specifically crafted glasses that can bestow this power. (As we will later see, the efficacy of these clothes and glasses is difficult to replicate in the real world. They are largely a gag, and wearers should know these do not guarantee your invisibility to all AI systems!)

Figure 3.2   An adversarial T-shirt in a controlled setting does not recognize the person wearing it. Courtesy of Zuxuan Wu

Adversarial examples are not restricted to image recognition systems. They are everywhere. The entire field of modern-day AI is prone to this malady. Smart systems that use audio commands, such as Amazon's Alexa, Apple's Siri, and Google's Assistant, can be fooled using adversarial examples. For instance, adversaries might play a modified sound, like Bach's Cello, but because it is interpreted differently by AI systems, they might open phones, dial phone numbers, or even browse specific websites because they are encoded with secret commands.

AI's ability to read natural language can be targeted, too. Consider the following phrases:

- *Sentence 1*: "Perfect performance by the actor"
- *Sentence 2*: "Spotless performance by the actor"

How would you classify the sentiment of both sentences? Do both evoke positive sentiments? Both negative?

According to BERT (short for Bidirectional Encoder Representations from Transformers), Google's 2019 state-of-the-art ML system for text processing, the first sentence conveys a positive sentiment, while the second conveys a negative sentiment. For the second sentence, researchers used specific algorithms to discover that substituting "spotless" for "perfect"—despite having the same meaning to humans—confused the text processing system. This starkly contrasts with the evasion used by Twitter's bot detector in Chapter 1, which appended random characters to a tweet. A visual inspection would have caught the alterations in the tweet, but adversarial examples are covert and not easily spotted by visual inspection. To us humans, both sentences are similar, but for the state-of-the-art ML system, the difference can be day and night.

Today, adversarial examples are one of the hottest areas in machine learning. A study of all the papers published in this area so far has identified Szegedy's and Goodfellow's works as the two most highly cited foundational works in AI Security. Subsequent papers in the field would later identify 2014—the year Szegedy's and Goodfellow's works were published—as the start of the adversarial machine learning revolution. But like most revolutions, the groundwork for worst-case adversarial inputs to evade machine learning was laid almost a decade earlier.

Research Disciplines Collide

If you had visited the Whistler Blackcomb Ski Resort in Whistler, British Columbia, from 1987 to 2013, you might have shared a ski lift with some of the most celebrated ML researchers in the world. It was no secret that the early organizers of the Neural Information Processing Systems (NeurIPS) conferences enjoyed powdery white snow, even noting that "The workshop program schedule allows time for informal discussions, skiing, and other winter sports."

While the plenary sessions were staid presentation-style affairs, the conference's workshops were more relaxed, resulting in no-holds-barred conversations between ML researchers from disparate fields, all liberally mixed with slaloming and schussing.

True to the conference's spirit, on a chilly Saturday morning in December 2007, computer security experts and ML researchers assembled at a nondescript ballroom at the Hilton Whistler Resort & Spa to participate in a workshop titled "Machine Learning in Adversarial Environments for Computer Security." Much of the work presented there revolved around evading the state-of-the-art email spam filters based on machine learning.

Battista Biggio's work appeared in the Whistler workshop. Biggio and his colleagues had been investigating a new evasion technique by email spammers and had proposed a method to prevent it. Spammers had been confronted with effective ML models that scanned the email's text for clues of spam. Phrases like "click here" or "Viagra," for example, caused the email to be blocked. So, spammers responded in the most logical way possible. They sent spam containing no text! Instead, they embedded an *image* containing advertisement text as a payload, readable to a human but not readily searchable by a computer.

As years passed, with a resurgent interest in neural networks, Biggio turned his attention to evading deep learning models. In 2013, independent of Szegedy and Goodfellow's work, Biggio's investigation led to the discovery of what is now called *adversarial examples*. But the routes that led to this independent discovery could not be more different or paradigmatic of the schism in the adversarial machine learning community.

Adversarial machine learning sits at the intersection of two separate fields: security and machine learning.

The security schism focuses on combating an adversary whose goal may be to thwart an ML-powered defense. Biggio and his collaborators pondered how to evade machine learning systems used in security contexts, much like how Biggio had originally evaded spam classifiers. That is why in his pioneering work, Biggio's discovery of adversarial examples was demonstrated to fool a machine learning system used to detect malicious emails.

On the other hand, the machine learning faction historically did not consider a subversive adversary. Szegedy and collaborators took a different route; their group studied how AI systems actually recognized images. There was no security angle when they started exploring. The adversary in adversarial ML is rooted in game theory, which broadly means someone who challenges the system with worst-case scenarios. Ironically, the paper that gripped the world's imagination about how unsafe and insecure the current deep learning system is did not start with a security angle.

Ultimately, Szegedy and Goodfellow's work attracted worldwide attention from researchers and the media. The jarring discrepancy between the visual appearance and the computer-generated outcome—*it looks like a panda, but an ImageNet-winning system thinks it's a gibbon!*—surprised observers. People wondered how AI got it so wrong. The image of the panda and the gibbon has since come to iconify adversarial failure modes in machine learning. To this day, virtually every discussion about adversarial machine learning begins with the image of a panda whose pixels have been perturbed to fool the AI system into thinking the image depicts a gibbon. A running joke in the adversarial machine learning community is that adversarial ML researchers have never actually seen a real picture of a gibbon, only the modified panda picture.

Another possible reason was the sheer popularity of those who wrote the paper. Szegedy was a rising star in the field of computer vision. He was instrumental in designing Google's deep learning system called Inception, which won the ImageNet competition in 2014. He would later gain more attention by finding ways to run deep learning at scale. Woj, Szegedy's colleague who goaded him to write the paper on adversarial examples, would go on to start OpenAI with another co-author, Ilya Sutskever. OpenAI would become a pioneering company in AI responsible for a series of breakthrough technologies, which *The New York Times* would call "one of the world's most ambitious artificial intelligence labs," attracting a $10 billion investment from Microsoft.

Goodfellow achieved more rarefied status. He independently discovered a fundamental technique called *generative adversarial networks* (GANs) after a night of celebration drinking at Les Trois Brasseurs pub in Montreal. (The pub was acknowledged in the paper for "stimulating creativity.") His work on GANs was so consequential that it led to a stream of accolades—*Fortune's* "40 Under-40" and MIT's "Innovators Under 35." When his advisor, Bengio, won the Turing Award, the Nobel prize equivalent for computer science, the prize committee specifically highlighted Bengio's contribution to generative systems, led by Goodfellow.

Because Goodfellow made foundational contributions to both GANs and adversarial machine learning, GANs are sometimes misconstrued as adversarial machine learning to this day when they are really two distinct fields with wispy relations. Since Goodfellow straddled these two fields seamlessly and achieved a rock-star status in both, his work became increasingly popular.

Essentially, the authors of the seminal work on adversarial examples became the who's who of AI. And coupled with the barn-burning interest in AI, the authors from the ML schism got more attention than those from the security side.

But this was not a case of warring factions fighting over who did it first, like Newton versus Leibnitz. Biggio told us it took only a simple email correspondence with Goodfellow to show their prior work. And *voilà*, things were fixed. No fuss. No mess. No drama. In fact, Biggio is thankful that Szegedy's paper has garnered more attention. It means more people are paying attention to the field of adversarial machine learning, and more people are researching how to secure it.

Today, Biggio is equally feted in the AI space. His work on adversarial machine learning was awarded the "Test of Time Award," the highest honor at the International Conference on Machine Learning in 2022, for shaping the field over the last decade.

Adversarial examples, ushered in by Biggio, Szegedy, and Goodfellow, represent one of the most well-probed areas in adversarial machine learning.

Blame Canada

In every field, there are simple questions for which there are no straightforward answers. Where do eels mate? Who is Homer? Why do bicycles stay upright? How frequently do prime numbers appear?

For AI security researchers, that question is, "Why do adversarial ML examples exist?"

There are myriad answers; we *kind of* know but also *kind of* do not know.

The first takeaway is that adversarial examples in ML models are more of a "feature" than a "bug." Researchers have demonstrated that ML models quite lazily learn concepts that are brittle indicators of the label or concept they learn. This behavior is not a corner case existing in only some AI systems applications. Rather, adversarial examples are a default property of AI systems. Why? It turns out that AI's building blocks promote the conditions for being easily tricked.

At the root is the misunderstood idea that an ML system somehow "learns" how to complete a task. Goodfellow likened many ML systems to a Potemkin village—faux constructions. From a distance, they appear impressive, yet they often do not stand up to close inspection. The quality of an ML model's construction is apparent when one presents data to it wholly inconsistent with what it has been trained on. For instance, if you had built an ML system to distinguish between apples and pears, asking the ML system to identify a tangerine is verboten. If your training set for the ML system consisted only of red apples, asking the system to identify, say, a green apple is verboten, too! Even with red apples, if your ML system sees only frontal views of apples, asking the system to identify a fruit from an overhead view will also cause the system to malfunction. Small deviations from the training data can cause large deviations in the model behavior. In other words, when one wanders beyond the broad streets of perfectly curated data to the alleys where the data contains nuance and corner cases, the illusion is dispelled, and the makeshift cardboard underpinnings of the Potemkin village are exposed. These "corner cases" abound in any machine learning system, and all the adversary needs to do is find them.

One of the rites of passage for any ML student is to build a model that can recognize handwritten numeric digits, such as one that might be used to read postal codes on an envelope—or, say, numbers on a bank check. A convenient dataset for this is provided by the National Institute of Standards and Technology (NIST) called the "Modified" NIST or MNIST dataset. It's a collection of small, grayscale images of handwritten numbers collected in the late 1990s from two unique sets of the population who do a lot of writing: high school students and American Census Bureau employees. Within MNIST are 60,000 grayscale 28x28 pixel images, with roughly 6,000 images of each digit, 0 through 9.

Recognizing numbers written in various handwriting styles has become a relatively easy feat for ML systems. For instance, researchers from the University of Virginia showed that an ML system could correctly identify the digits 9,979 out of 10,000 times on average (a 0.21 percent error rate). MNIST is largely considered a toy dataset now.

Even for such accurate systems, you can trivially generate adversarial examples that look like a number 5 to you and me, but to an ML system, it would look like a 1 (see Figure 3-3). Imagine someone handing you a check for $5, but it is really worth only $1 in the eyes of an AI system.

Figure 3.3 This looks like a number 5 to humans but is a number 1 to a machine learning system.

The *manifold hypothesis* explains this intriguing phenomenon of how small changes in images can make a large difference in AI's perception. In machine learning parlance, a manifold is a little bit like the population distribution of Canada. Canada is large—3.9 million square miles—making it larger than the United States and China and twice the size of Europe. For a country this big, Canada has a meager 37 million people. In comparison, the United States is 10 times more populated! To put this in perspective, California alone has more people than all of Canada. Imagine the entire landmass of the United States consisting only of Californians; Canada is even more sparsely populated!

Naively, one might expect a country's population centers to be uniformly distributed across the country, but that is not the case at all for Canada. Ninety percent of Canadians live within 100 miles of the U.S. border. Pictured on a map, that narrow strip of geographic borderland where most Canadians reside is a sort of population manifold.

How do population distributions relate to adversarial examples? It's about the boundaries. The Canada-U.S. *political* boundary is the longest international boundary in the world and "classifies" people as being either U.S. or Canadian citizens. One-third of the 4,000-mile stretch separating Canada from the continental United States is comprised of a straightish line—the 49th parallel—a boundary defined by treaties.

A machine learning model creates a *decision* boundary defined by its training data. This boundary is formed empirically by a learning algorithm that attempts to separate the images by the labels assigned to them. And in machine learning, that decision boundary is drawn very closely around the data distribution. Hence, almost every data point lives very close to the decision boundary!

For example, in deep learning (neural network) models, the decision boundary begins its life as a randomly initialized separation between outcomes. As the algorithm begins to compare the labeled training images of 5s and 1s to that initial guess, the boundary is pushed, pulled, merged, or separated to incrementally improve the separation. After the model's lifetime of training, the decision boundary becomes a sort-of shrink-wrapped fit around the data distribution. Such a boundary includes many dimples, pockets, nooks, and crannies that attempt (imperfectly) to conform to the data. Because the data does not live in a straight line, that decision boundary may differ from the straight line separating much of the United States and Canada. And this presents an opening to an adversary.

To confuse the classifier, an adversary only needs to move an image of a 5 to the other side of the boundary, where all images are recognized as 1s! For instance, the images shown in Figure 3-4 might both look like 5s to a human, but for a deep learning model trained on MNIST data, the one on the left is a 5, and the one on the right is a 1.

Figure 3.4 The Image on the left is unaltered and recognized as 5. The one on the right is an adversarial example and recognized as a 1. If you squint your eye, you may notice it is fuzzy and grainier.

But how do you "move" the 5 from one side of the boundary to the other? The adversary generates a specific noise-like pattern and adds it to the original number 5 image. The resulting grainier, subtly perturbed image (rightmost image in Figure 3-5) still looks like number 5 to humans but will be classified as 1 because of the additive adversarial pattern. The resulting image is the "adversarial example" because the subtle yet specific adversarial noise pattern we added pushes the 5 to the 1 region. It's not just *any* noise. It's very *specific* noise that corresponds to the shortest path for a border crossing. Adding the specific "adversarial noise" to the original image subtly changes the original image but drastically changes the prediction.

Figure 3.5 This is the specific noise added to "move" it across the decision boundary.

The same concept works everywhere.

- Want to confuse an AI-powered X-ray system into misrecognizing a malignant scan as benign (see Figure 3-6)? Add adversarial noise.
- Want to confuse an AI-powered audio transcription service that mistranscribes "What is the time?" to "Cancel the meeting"? Add adversarial noise.

Adversarial examples are present in all ML models.

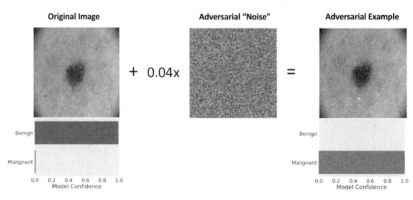

Figure 3.6 Adding adversarial noise to medical image scans has the potential to confuse AI systems. Here the AI system changes its diagnosis from benign to malignant after adding the adversarial noise. Courtesy of Samuel G. Finlayson

A definitive explanation for the existence of adversarial examples, like the gibbon-panda pairs that result from only tiny perturbations, is still a matter of debate among experts. But, no matter which of the theories you subscribe to, a key question is this: How does an adversary discover the precise pattern of pixels to formulate the attack?

Turns out, there is an easy recipe. The same recipe is used to teach ML systems to be smart.

The Intelligent Wiggle-Jiggle

Niles:	The atmosphere has to be absolutely perfect.
Frasier:	Good point. Let's begin with the lighting.
Niles:	Warmer. [Frasier turns the switch a tad to the right.]
Niles:	Warmer. [Frasier turns the dial more to the right.]
Niles:	A little cooler. [Frasier turns the dial to the left.]
Niles:	A touch warmer. [Frasier turns the dial right again.]
Niles:	A hair back. [Frasier gives up and goes over to the drinks cabinet while Niles, still concentrating on the lighting, keeps on talking.]
Niles:	No, no, a hair the other way. No, a touch warmer. Perfect.

— Frasier, Season 4, Episode 4

Three things make up a machine learning system: input data, output label, and the parameters in the middle. The parameters are something like an AI system's dials and levers, which are tuned in a specific way so that the input is mapped to the appropriate output.

Let's pretend you want to train a machine learning system that can distinguish apples from pears. First, you would collect hundreds or thousands of images of apples and pears and then provide labels for each image. You'd arrange these data in pairs, so each image has a corresponding label. For example, using (image-label) pairs, we might collate pictures of apples and annotate them as "apples" and pictures of pears and annotate them as "pears." The machine's learning task is to fit the parameters of a model so that it can reproduce the correct output label for each input image. Many modern machine learning systems depend on an algorithm called *gradient descent* to tune the parameters to be *just right* to achieve the objective.

Before training, the parameters do not define a model representing the data particularly well. When presented with a training image of an apple, the parameters might initially be wired to report "pear." Because we've annotated the image with the correct label, "apple," we can measure the error in the answer. This is where gradient descent kicks in. The error *gradient* serves as Goldilocks' cry of "too hot!" signaling the model parameters to adjust their settings slightly so that the model will now report "apple."

The error gradient is quite similar to finding the right temperature setting in your shower. We all have an ideal shower temperature that is the perfect mix of hot and cold water in our muscle memory. Now imagine being in a new bathroom trying to figure out that combination. First, you might tilt the knob to the right (too hot!) and then left (too cold!); after a few minutes and dozens of wiggles and jiggles, you discover just the right temperature setting for you. That's what happens during training models using gradient descent: the error gradient adjusts increases or decreases the parameters until the bulk of the annotated images are classified correctly.

As it turns out, gradient descent, which guides researchers when training a machine learning system, is also how attackers can find adversarial examples that evade them. But there is one important difference: rather than applying the error gradient signal ("too hot!") to adjust the model parameters, attackers use the error signal to adjust the input image.

When attacking an ML system, the adversary begins by choosing the output they want to arrive at, such as confusing an image of an apple as a pear. The adversary allows the ML model parameters to remain at their perfectly tuned settings. Without modification, the model correctly labels the image of an apple as "apple." To the adversary, this is actually an error! "Too hot!" The error gradient flows unchanged through the dials and knobs (the ML model parameters) to the input image and suggests precisely how to modify the color and intensity of pixels to arrive at the adversary's goal "just right" so that the ML system can call it a pear.

Essentially, by using gradient descent, the attacker can ask the ML model, "How should I change this image of an apple so that you, the ML model, label it as a pear?" The attacker can wiggle and jiggle the input until just the right output is achieved.

Kendra Albert, technology lawyer superstar from Harvard Law School, is one of the earliest scholars to study the legal implications of adversarial machine learning. Albert likens adversarial machine learning to the card game *Go Fish*. This is how the game goes: a player asks an opponent for a card, and if the opponent has the card, the opponent must hand it (or them) over or tell the player to "go fish" in the stack for another card. By paying attention to the answers provided by the opponent, the player can incrementally learn what cards are in the opponent's hand. Similarly, attackers can query the ML model to determine how it responds to the image that the attacker has constructed. By paying attention to the ML model's answers, the adversary can adjust their strategy—similar to the *Go Fish* game.

At this point, you may be thinking, why would the ML model reveal answers to an adversary? That's because an ML model cannot distinguish the intent behind the query (are you friend or foe?). The ML model answers truthfully *all the time*. This provides valuable feedback and is a signal to the attacker to refine subsequent queries. Using the feedback, the adversary can course-correct and make modifications until the ML model is eventually fooled.

This simple technique to attack AI systems has curious consequences. For one, an attacker can begin with *any* input and use this approach to modify it into something that the ML system recognizes. For instance, the static noise image (on the left side of Figure 3-7) has been modified "just right" so the that the model actually believes it to be a 1. The image (on the right) has been modified "just right" using gradient descent so that the system misrecognizes it as the digit 6.

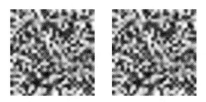

Figure 3.7 The attacker can start with any image and modify it to something the ML system recognizes. The image on the left is recognized as a 1. The image on the right is recognized as a 6.

The generated adversarial noise works beyond the digital domain. Google researchers confused a deep learning system by printing an adversarial patch of a toaster and placing it on a table with a banana (see Figure 3-8). A picture of the banana with the adversarial patch was sufficient to confuse the deep learning system into thinking it was a picture of a toaster.

MIT researchers took it a step further. In lieu of stickers, they 3D printed a turtle with a specific texture. Humans would instantly recognize it as a turtle. It has a turtle shape and, for all intents and purposes, looks like a turtle. In 2017, Google's AI system quite confidently misrecognized the turtle as a rifle. Imagine the consequences if the reverse played out where an adversary 3D prints guns that are misrecognized as something benign.

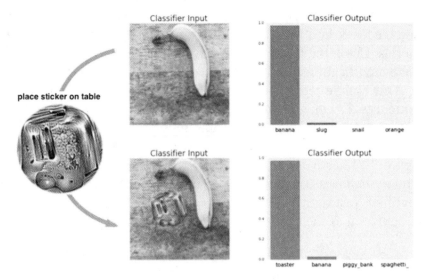

Figure 3.8   Adversarial noise can be printed on a physical patch to confuse AI systems. Courtesy of Tom B. Brown and Dandelion Mané

Thus far, we have assumed the attacker knows everything about the ML model—its parameters, inputs, and outputs needed to attack it. Indeed, many ML models are built upon open-source software, with their internal parameters published for academic transparency and reproducibility. This is not surprising. An influential academic paper in 2007 strongly advocated for this approach in its title, "The Need for Open Source Software in Machine Learning." The authors of this influential paper went on to lead academic research groups at Facebook, Google, Apple, and Amazon and brought this philosophy with them. So, it is often the case that when a machine learning system is released, at least some details about the machine learning system are known.

But what happens when an attacker does not know these details of the ML system?

Bargain-Bin Models Will Do

Nicolas Papernot is a magnoludovicien.

That's what students at France's most prestigious and notoriously difficult prep school, Lycée Louis-Le-Grand, are called. Located in Paris's Latin Quarter between the Sorbonne and College De France, the school's alumni include all the French intelligentsia you could think of: Molière, Voltaire, Hugo, Degas, Sarte, Baudelaire. Half of all the Field Medalists from France, the Nobel Prize equivalent in mathematics, come from this prep school. Unlike schools in the United States, where the kids go through a patchwork of different classes with complicated schedules, students at this public school have a straightforward but grueling schedule: 4 hours of advanced math in the morning and 4 hours of theoretical physics in the afternoon. That's it. Here, Papernot would solve worksheet after worksheet of calculus, algebra, and probability theory that would later prove useful to him.

As the school website reads, "You don't enter Louis-le-Grand for its name, but going there can help make one." And Nicolas Papernot most definitely made a name for himself in adversarial machine learning.

But the road to his fame was far from obvious. He moved to Penn State University for grad school, where he first dipped his toes in research with securing databases. The research was moving, but he wasn't finding the big impact he was seeking. Patrick

McDaniel, Papernot's PhD advisor, gave Papernot space to find his way. In March 2015, McDaniel had just returned from a visit to Google to get an idea of how the industry is moving with regard to AI. By 2015, Google had started investing heavily in deep learning to capitalize on the AI trend, with acquisitions such as DeepMind— the company that built AlphaGo. McDaniel, who has a knack for chasing down good ideas before they become the next big thing, wanted to get ahead of the curve and see how researchers can shape the AI trend.

It was a Friday afternoon, and McDaniel had to walk over to the other side of the campus for an errand and asked Papernot to join him to discuss this new deep learning trend that Google was investing so much in. McDaniel was a security heavyweight, but his forte was in "traditional" computer security like protecting networks from intrusions. So, he asked Papernot if he could learn the ropes of deep learning and come back to his office on Monday to discuss their security.

Papernot did what anyone does when their boss gives them two days to learn something totally new. He turned to YouTube lectures and devoured all the lectures by Geoffrey Hinton, one of the winners of the 2012 ImageNet challenge. (Papernot would later become Hinton's colleague at the University of Toronto.)

But the more Papernot learned about deep learning, the more he discovered it was just his prep school math repackaged. He didn't just learn the basics; he also found ways to break the system. When he met McDaniel on Monday, McDaniel was astounded how someone could go from not knowing about deep learning to breaking it, in two days. He asked Papernot to drop everything and pursue how to attack AI systems.

When an attacker knows the internal workings of the machine learning system, attack algorithms based on gradient descent provide a straightforward recipe to generate adversarial examples. An attack that requires full knowledge of an ML system is called a *white-box* or *full-knowledge* attack. Because companies held back releasing the details of their ML models, attackers have increasingly had to work under a *black-box* or *zero-knowledge* setting when little is known about the underlying machine learning system. Much like the tit-for-tat between spammers and spam filters, the challenge to do more with less has only motivated attackers to find a way in.

For instance, you cannot access the parameters behind the facial recognition system used to unlock your phone. You can only present your face to the camera to receive its verdict; you are either signed in or denied access. This is a black-box situation where you can present only inputs and observe outputs.

But there is another way to make gradient descent attacks. And it came from Papernot's insight that adversarial examples transfer across algorithms. The concept is not unlike the standardized exam scene in the United States. Every year, 2 million high school students take the Scholastic Aptitude Test (SAT) for college admissions. If the SAT is not your cup of tea, you can be like the 1.7 million students that take an alternative exam called the ACT, which is administered by a different company.

The SAT and ACT are different exams with distinct scoring systems administered by different organizations. However, because both are used for college admissions, they test language, math, and science knowledge. If you do well on the SAT, chances are you will also do well on the ACT. In fact, the tests are so comparable that the companies administering them have published a table to convert one exam score to the other. In other words, preparation and performance for one exam transfer to another.

Papernot made the remarkable discovery that adversarial examples against one kind of ML model transfer readily to another algorithm. Szegedy observed that the same adversarial example could fool multiple instances of the same kind of algorithm. But Papernot went one step further. He showed that the same adversarial example could fool different algorithms. In other words, if you have an adversarial example that fooled algorithm A, it is likely to fool a completely different algorithm B.

For instance, Papernot found that adversarial examples discovered on one algorithm called *support vector machines* for image recognition are also very likely to fool a second image recognition model powered by *deep neural networks* or *random-forest* or *k-nearest neighbor* algorithms. Completely different ML models are fundamentally vulnerable to the same adversarial examples.

This was a stunning result with multiple ramifications, as we will see in this and subsequent chapters. Why this happens remains very much open to debate among machine learning experts.

How does the *transferability property* of ML help an attacker in a black-box setting? Simply put, an attacker can first replicate the behavior of a black-box model through a model that's in their control to create. This new model, since it is in the attacker's control comes with all the information needed to launch whitebox gradient attacks: inputs, outputs, and parameters. Using white box attacks that rely on gradient descent, the adversary can produce adversarial examples. But these are adversarial examples on the replicated model; not the original model, you might say. This is where Papernot's transferability result comes into play: there is a good chance that the adversarial examples found on the replicated model will work against the original model.

In practice, the process looks like this: let's assume that the attacker wants to fool a bank's handwritten digit-recognizer software used to identify numbers in checks. Obviously, the attacker does not know the details of this model, but the attacker can effectively *steal* the functionality by creating a replica for which it *does* know the details.

First, the attacker queries the bank's model with sample input handwritten digits and records the model's responses. These become the pairs of inputs and outputs required to train a surrogate model. The surrogate model could be any type, but for convenience, the attacker chooses the one most efficient for gradient-based white-box attacks. Training the model requires time and computing resources. This already constitutes a *model-stealing* attack.

But the attacker goes further. With the surrogate model at hand, the attacker is now in a white-box setting. Since the attacker designed the surrogate, the attacker knows the model type and the model parameters and can generate adversarial examples freely using gradient descent techniques. Now, the attacker has adversarial examples that fool their stolen copy, the surrogate model.

Thanks to the magic of Papernot's transferability finding, the attacker must only replay the adversarial example to the bank's original model. And *voilà*, the bank's model is also tricked.

Interestingly enough, it matters little if the surrogate model type differs from the target model. Transferability works *better* when both share a common architecture, but strikingly, Papernot showed that there is always transferability, even when the target model is one kind of ML algorithm and the surrogate is a totally different algorithm. Furthermore, the surrogate model need not be state-of-the-art! Surrogate models can be quite simple and rather cheap to train—the machine learning equivalent of a model discovered in a bargain bin that is used just once to generate adversarial examples and then discarded.

Black-box attacks on machine learning systems are one of the most consequential issues for the security of ML. They disrupt the notion that simply hiding the ML algorithms behind a gated system would provide sufficient security. In our conversations with organizations, we have routinely heard teams claim that their ML models are secure because they are "internal only" and that the details of the ML algorithms are proprietary.

With machine learning, there is no "internal only." If the user can use your ML powered system, they can replicate it. If they can replicate it, they can very much attack it. Transferability results explose the security by obscurity fallacy.

But why does all of this matter? Who are the adversaries that would utilize adversarial examples to trick ML systems anyway? And who are their targets?

For Whom the Adversarial Example Bell Tolls

Physical adversarial examples like a stop sign and adversarial sweatshirts that fool computer vision systems get all the billing, but buyer of this trend, beware.

Adversarial wearables such as T-shirts, glasses, and hats are tested on very few people, and almost always on those conducting the research. For instance, the sweatshirt mentioned at the beginning of the chapter was tested on five people; the Mila Jokovich glasses were tested on three. But this has not stopped the media from posing this as a solution to the surveillance age. A news publication touted an adversarial cap as a tool that "can fool facial recognition software into thinking anyone is anyone else." What the news publication failed to highlight was that the researchers had tested the attack on exactly one person wearing the cap. That is not exactly a strong guarantee they will actually allow you to slip past the panopticon in various lighting conditions or different skin tones, gender, and body shapes. This is a case of overtrust, too—overtrust that physical adversarial examples always work.

Now for the next question that might be on your mind: should you worry that an adversary will wield adversarial examples against you? To answer this, we need to unpack the impact of launching adversarial examples and understand what kind of adversary would launch them.

We have highlighted the *impact* of launching adversarial examples:

- *They are subtle*: You cannot visually identify an adversarial image.
- *They are specific*: The adversary can tune the image to be misrecognized for exactly the desired outcome.
- *They are ever-present:* Adversarial examples are features common to all machine learning models today, rather than bugs present in just a few.

When considering what kind of adversary would employ adversarial examples, it is also instructive to understand the *cost* of launching these attacks. Cost in terms of knowledge and skillset is one dimension. After all, if you need PhDs in machine learning and computer security to launch these kinds of attacks, it would certainly limit the number of people capable of disrupting AI systems. Another dimension is, of course, cost in terms of the economic forbearance for launching these attacks. If the adversary had to spend more money to launch these attacks than they profited from them, it would not make economic sense to launch them. The adversary would be better off finding another path to dupe their target.

It is interesting to note how the tools to launch these adversarial attacks are not locked away in a secret vault. They are available for anyone to use. That is a good thing because defenders know what to look for if an adversary leverages these tools. From IBM's Adversarial Robustness Toolkit to Microsoft's Counterfit to Baidu's Paddle-Paddle, tools to evade machine learning systems are commonplace. No PhD or math background is required to use these tools; just a basic understanding of computers will do. There's a learning curve, but it's certainly not nearly as difficult as crafting your own attacks from scratch.

Black-box attacks on machine learning systems are becoming increasingly easier to mount. You can make a knock-off model that functions like the original most of the time for less than the cost of a large pizza.

This unique combination of high impact—subtle, specific, and ever-present—and low barriers to entry, both in terms of cost and skillset, can be concerning. But not for you, the reader.

The good news is that the kind of adversary employing adversarial examples is unlikely to target the general population. Why would an adversary go through the trouble of mastering machine learning, understanding the ropes of adversarial machine learning, generating stickers, and then placing them on stop signs in the hope of causing a car to fail? Instead, can an attacker just rent a billboard and flash a yield sign?

In reality, your AI-powered car is more likely to fail *without* any adversary intervention: inclement weather, a flock of seagulls, or even a truck parked on the side of the road. There were 273 reported Tesla crashes involving its AI-powered Autopilot system in 2021. While we do not know the exact causes of these crashes, we can take an educated guess that none of these were caused by adversarial stickers on a stop sign.

In the same vein, one need not worry about a smart speaker, Siri, or Alexa being duped by audio adversarial examples. These attacks are quite finicky and hard to pull off in the real world because of background noise. There are benign ways to fool your smart speaker. For instance, saying "Cocaine noodles" triggered Google Home speakers because it sounded like "Okay, Google."

Alexa may be more likely duped by a *South Park* episode that used a character named Alexa, doubling as the smart speaker wake word. According to reports, if you had watched that episode in the same room as your Alexa smart speaker, you would have ended up with added weird items in your Amazon cart and an alarm set for 7 a.m.

Indeed, the general population is more likely to face threats from run-of-the-mill malicious entities who are more prone to getting your credit card number via scam text messages. Most of us should be safe from adversarial examples because adversaries have other tools in their arsenal to profit from us.

So, why did NSCAI—the all-star commission of AI experts we learned about in Chapter 1—warn about attacks on AI systems?

The motivation for using something subtle, specific, and ever-present comes more into focus if we look beyond consumer cars to higher-stakes opportunities. For example, consider an AI-controlled military aircraft tested by the U.S. Air Force aboard the Lockheed U-2 "Dragon Lady" spy plane in December 2020. Or consider Russian autonomous surveillance vehicles used in Syria in 2019. While the threat of adversaries to the general population via adversarial examples is low, the *possibility* of that occurring to high-stakes entities has generated marked interest and early thinking for governments. The presence of a sophisticated, algorithmically capable adversary is plausible, even if the scenario is extreme.

The U.S. government should prepare for such threats, given that its adversaries are girding their loins. As we saw in Chapter 1, China has overtly indicated an interest in adversarial machine learning. The Russian Defense Ministry recently created an AI-specific division "to intensify work on the use of artificial intelligence technologies in the interests of creating models of weapons for military and special equipment."

It should come as no surprise that in its final report, NSCAI dedicated an entire chapter to adversarial AI, writing "even small manipulations of these data sets or algorithms can lead to consequential changes for how AI systems operate." Those small manipulations the NSCAI is referring to are adversarial examples.

The changes from these manipulations can have far-reaching consequences. When speaking at the Air Force Association's 2021 Air, Space & Cyber Conference about the points in the machine learning life cycle that could be affected by an adversary, Lt. General Mary O'Brien, Deputy Chief of Staff for Intelligence, Surveillance, Reconnaissance and Cyber Effects, said, "If our adversary injects uncertainty into any part of that process, we're kind of dead in the water on what we wanted the AI to do for us."

That's the key problem with adversarial examples. Is that a picture of a panda or a gibbon? It can inject uncertainty and shake our trust in AI systems. If weaponized, it can be a decisive advantage to thwart our adversary's AI system.

But adversarial examples are far from the only way to corrupt AI systems. There is an even more accessible and impactful way.

Chapter 4
Here's Something I Found on the Web

"Welcome to side hustles I recommend trying—part one." Sarah Frank launched her TikTok video series on July 23, 2021. Her mission was to help her fellow teenagers earn extra money. Frank posted her first video in a series called #sarahsidehustles in front of a whiteboard decorated with motivational quotes, folder cubbies, and picture frames with myriad photos tastefully accented with feathers. She promised to provide ideas her listeners could use to earn extra cash without resorting to delivering for DoorDash or driving for Uber. And her very first recommendation caused a ripple effect.

Fourteen days later, a confused Cornell PhD student took to Twitter to understand why women were flocking to his academic survey about social comparisons and money. His data showed a wild skew in responses that made him question his results: 91 percent of respondents were female. Others also reported skewed data in their own studies, including an assistant professor at Virginia Tech and a doctoral student at Yale. Of the 60 respondents to the Yale survey, only two were men.

In a Twitter comment, one poster noted Frank's recent video on TikTok, which had now gone viral. "This may be far-fetched, but given the timing, the virality of the video, and the user's follower demographics.. . ." Notably, Frank's TikTok video included the hashtag #prolific.

Prolific is a marketplace for scientists to recruit survey participants. Used by researchers anywhere from Oxford to Stanford, Prolific helps scholars collect high-quality responses from its pool of more than 150,000 participants worldwide. In return for the responders' time, Prolific compensates them to the tune of $6.50 per hour.

Frank's TikTok video for side-hustle hot tips included the suggestion to enroll in Prolific and fill out surveys for extra income. With more than 4 million views flooding in, the video went viral for a very specific demographic. Throngs of teenage and young adult girls, Frank's target audience, rushed to Prolific to fill out surveys, resulting in 30,000 new signups on the platform in a matter of days. It became so popular that many flocked to the platform from word-of-mouth referrals—Google search activity on July 24, 2021, showed a positive uptick for the term *prolific surveys*.

The surge in signups, primarily from teens and 20-something females, skewed the expected demographics of the carefully designed research surveys. If the researchers were not careful about who they expected to answer their survey, their study would have been tainted by the sudden surge of women—an unintended capture bias. Prolific's co-founder and CTO, Phelim Bradley, told *Verge* that the viral TikTok video disrupted 4,600 studies. Prolific later refunded studies significantly affected by the video and put tools in place to handle these kinds of surges.

Just as a teenager with a 56-second video can disrupt thousands of scientific studies by corrupting the data used in its research, a motivated adversary can disrupt state-of-the-art AI systems by corrupting the data used to train its models. Further, since most of the data behind these AI systems is freely available from the Internet, what are the security implications of using open data for critical AI systems?

Bad Data = Big Problem

The number-one attack on AI systems that organizations worry about is *not* the sticker attack for traffic signs.

That's what we found when we spoke to multiple organizations using machine learning: from startups to Fortune 500–sized companies to governments worldwide. It was the first survey of the kind, and we roped in AI engineers and security analysts to get a comprehensive snapshot of the state of adversarial machine learning from an industry perspective.

The top worry for organizations we found, by an overwhelming majority, was poisoning attacks. These attacks deliberately feed the ML system bad data to change how the model behaves from conception. A follow-up study by other researchers confirms that in a survey of 139 organizations, poisoning is top of mind, especially pronounced in fields like IT security, where adversaries are prevalent.

But, even without an active adversary, feeding bad data can cause considerable damage to an AI system and cause business loss. For example, consider Unity, the popular gaming software that powers video games like *Pokemon Go*, *Call of Duty*, and more than half of all mobile games. Unity heavily invested in machine learning across the board to improve gameplay. But, in May 2022, it suffered more than $100 million in losses, in part because one of its AI systems ingested "bad data from a large customer."

The key issue is that once the model is trained on data, the die has been cast. Discovered that your input data is corrupt and want to fix your model? Today, the only viable option is to start over—to retrain the model from scratch. This requires a spate of resources: costly compute resources and developers' time and focus away from creating new features. Indeed, Unity's CEO told investors, "As a consequence of reprioritizing work in our teams to thoroughly address the resiliency and data training issues, we delayed the launch of certain revenue-driving features." Unity later fixed the issue in a subsequent quarter.

The problem of data quality management is further complicated by an adversary attempting to actively inject bad data into the system.

Poisoning attacks caught the tech world's imagination with Microsoft's Tay Twitter bot, which had to be decommissioned within 24 hours of its launch because Internet trolls poisoned its input data by interacting with it. Tay has become a textbook example of poisoning attacks—invoked by researchers as a cautionary tale of how adversaries can manipulate state-of-the-art ML systems by injecting them with bad data.

A quick reminder before you plumb into this chapter: an adversary in adversarial machine learning is anyone who violates the assumptions upon which ML systems were built. An adversary may not always refer to a hacker in a hoodie, nor does it always require a PhD. It may be a person wanting to fool ad trackers or to hoodwink a public organization to prove a point.

Your AI Is Powered by Ghost Workers

You may think that building the actual machine learning algorithm is the hardest part of developing a machine learning system. That is largely due to how it is advertised: "advanced," "intelligent," and "powered by math."

However, the most difficult part of creating AI systems for most organizations is getting data in the right format to the algorithm's doorstep for processing. The key to good machine learning performance is good data. There is a common trope that "data is the new oil." But, striking it rich in data is much more than finding the right drilling location in a west Texas prairie. Finding a data source that can be tapped again and again is only part of the challenge. To fuel the applications you care about, data must also be refined. There are many steps engineers must take to get the data in the right format. Data needs to be collected and then cleaned, annotated, and formatted correctly so that it can be ready for ingestion by the algorithm.

Each data source and subsequent refinement process introduces complexity in product development. Indeed, ML engineers from

Google, in a reflection piece entitled "Machine Learning: The High Interest Credit Card of Technical Debt," noted that data dependencies cost even more than code dependencies, even if the data source is freely available. They stress that it is "dangerous" to think of open source datasets as "coming for free," and organizations can "incur massive ongoing maintenance costs" to make and keep such systems operational. "Even the addition of one or two seemingly innocuous data dependences can slow further progress," they highlighted.

One of the most tedious steps for data refinement is annotating or labeling data. This step is where, for example, each image is tagged with the right label. ImageNet, a corpus of millions of annotated images, was a key enabler to power the deep learning revolution because, although the labels were imperfect, someone did the work to label them. That someone? Gig workers in crowdsourcing platforms like Amazon's Mechanical Turk where respondents are compensated at a "cost-effective" rate. A study found that Amazon Mechanical Turks, for example, are paid to the tune of $3 per hour to annotate reams of images. Anthropologist and MacArthur "Genius" Fellow, Mary Gray coined the term *ghost work* in her seminal book of the same name, to describe the on-demand human workers who are often involved in doing the grunt work in the digital world.

Tesla, for instance, has close to 1,000 data labelers on its staff to improve its Autopilot feature. This is how Tesla described that task in a job posting: "Labeled data is the critical ingredient for training powerful deep neural networks, which help drive the Tesla vehicles autonomously. In this role, you will work with a user interface to label images for cars, lanes, street signs, etc." Facebook previously hired hundreds of data labelers from India to go through Facebook posts and classify the post's subject—such as whether the post related to food—and ascertain the post's intention (inspirational, joke, event planning, and so on). Smart speakers and voice-activated assistants—be it Amazon's Alexa, Google Assistant, Microsoft's Cortana, or Apple's Siri—have reportedly sent a small portion of the interaction with the speaker the companies' employees and contractors worldwide from India to Ireland for annotation.

The incentives for ghost workers are often misplaced. When a data labeler is paid by the task—and at an embarrassingly low wage of pennies to label each item—their focus is to maximize the rewards and the number of tasks completed. Consequently, the quality may fall by the wayside.

Researchers from MIT found that the top 10 datasets used to benchmark AI systems are riddled with errors. For instance, you might guess Figure 4-1 is of someone wearing jeans, but as researchers at MIT discovered, the label in ImageNet was incorrectly assigned *by a ghost worker* as a "bathtub."

Figure 4.1 This picture of a person wearing jeans was incorrectly tagged as "bathtub" on ImageNet, one of many such mislabelings.
labelerrors.com / https://labelerrors.com/ / last accessed January 10, 2023.

Sometimes, these incorrect labels in ImageNet are dark and troubling. Researchers found a picture of a smiling woman sporting a bikini that was tagged by crowd workers in ImageNet as a "slattern, slut, slovenly woman, trollop." A picture of actress Sigourney Weaver was tagged as a "hermaphrodite." A photo of an overweight person was tagged as a "loser."

These misannotated or maliciously annotated datasets have serious downstream consequences. At best, as MIT researchers found, algorithms trained on these tainted datasets do not generalize well and provide an overly confident picture of their utility to society. In the worst case, these mistakes can propagate the biases of those annotating the datasets, leading models to propagate the unparliamentary name-calling captured by the original label.

ImageNet, which sparked the AI revolution and symbolized the epitome of quality, eventually fell from grace, owing to a parade of problems: improperly tagged data, indecorous images, and unclear licensing. At one point, more than 600,000 images—half its database—were culled.

The reality is that ghost workers are propping up the entire AI scaffolding as they continue to annotate datasets. These erroneously tagged datasets can seriously impede leadership decisions with tragic consequences if used in critical areas such as finance, healthcare, or defense. Imagine a computer vision system targeting a minaret because it was misrecognized as a missile because of faulty annotation.

ML researchers have begun to ask whether we can free machine learning's dependency from the hard work of annotating datasets. If human-annotated data has become so costly and fraught with errors, why not teach machines to learn from unannotated datasets and cut out the human-in-the-loop completely? Tesla took to this philosophy by laying off hundreds of data labelers in favor of automatic labeling software.

But, as it turns out, this proposed solution is very much like attempting to slay the hydra—when you cut off its head, two others sprout up in its place.

Your AI Is Powered by Vampire Novels

Natural language processing (NLP) is the arm of machine learning dedicated to teaching algorithms to reason about spoken or written language. For instance, when you ask Alexa, "Where is the nearest Walmart?" your device first needs to understand that this is a question. Next, it must understand that Walmart is a retail store and that "where" and "near" refer to distance. Then, Alexa must put all these pieces together, calculate the distance to various Walmart stores from your location, and select the nearest one.

In NLP, annotating a complete body of text, even in a single language like English, is nearly impossible. For instance, "We saw her duck" could refer to the sighting of either a woman's pet waterfowl or the collective act of seeing someone lower their head. Language has too much nuance and context to objectively label every sentence. So, without a body of text that provides annotations similar to what ImageNet provided for computer vision, NLP researchers had to solve the problem differently.

NLP researchers recast the problem by turning to advances in *unsupervised* learning. In this AI paradigm, machine learning systems do not need large volumes of annotated data. Instead, researchers use huge amounts of *unannotated* data first to "pre-train" the system to be familiar with the basic concepts of language. With that foundation, a generic pre-trained model can be subsequently fine-tuned to specialized custom tasks, such as rating movie reviews, understanding Internet search queries, or calculating distances to the nearest Walmart.

Fine-tuning is a simple shortcut humans use all the time. Imagine you would like a specific color chair. One option is to buy the wood, buy the required tools, make the chair, and then paint it the color of your choice. Alternatively, you could buy a white chair from Ikea and paint it. The second option is the pretraining/fine-tuning regime. Essentially, researchers build a generic task over tomes of unannotated data; all one needs to do is simply customize it for the task at hand.

So, where does one find large volumes of unannotated text? The Internet, of course.

With close to 6 million articles in the English language alone, Wikipedia is the world's largest open encyclopedia, encapsulating 20 gigabytes of compressed, open-domain knowledge for researchers to feed into the hungry algorithms for pretraining. One can visit dumps.wikimedia.org and download the entire Wikipedia exactly as it existed at that time, no questions asked. Wikipedia is not only free, but it is also relatively high-quality. Unlike the poor annotation that plagued ImageNet, an army of regimented wiki editors ensures the quality and consistency of the input data to the NLP algorithms.

Another added advantage is that the same Wikipedia article is frequently translated into various languages—for instance, the article on Jesus Christ has been translated into 253 languages—which also helps ML algorithms learn language translation tasks.

Online books also provided a fruitful source. In the BookCorpus dataset, researchers downloaded thousands of books from a site called Smashwords.com—everything ranging from romance novellas to young adult fiction to vampire stories.

Who knew that AI was powered, in part, by vampire novels?

Wikipedia articles on UFOs and online vampire novels are not the sole sources of text that power information-hungry algorithms. Nearly the *entire* Internet is used. Common Crawl is a nonprofit organization that regularly captures snapshots of large swaths of the Internet and makes them publicly available. Each crawl consists of a snapshot of the Internet, frozen in time, consisting of trillions of URLs, covering everything from Reddit posts to restaurant menus. This Internet time capsule may be used directly to train models or indirectly when other popular ML datasets are distilled from it. These derived datasets—with names like LAION-5B, the Pile, and CC-100 that appropriately sound like the custom parts of a gearhead to soup up their performance vehicle—are key ingredients to the powerful and impressive chatbots, text-to-images, and translation models that have fired up the public imagination.

Of course, not all machine learning is powered by open datasets. There are many sectors where open source is not the norm. Healthcare organizations use ML models trained on electronic health records and are kept private. Banks use ML that is trained on its users' credit card transactions—locked down data. But, by and large, most of today's cutting-edge models and compelling applications are built on open-source Internet data.

In 2018, Google developed BERT, a general-purpose text processing model that produced state-of-the-art results for various language tasks such as comprehension, text generation, and sentiment analysis. It caught everyone's attention, with *The New York Times* writing, "BERT's arrival punctuated a significant development in artificial intelligence."

What could possibly go wrong by reading things from the Internet?

Don't Believe Everything You Read on the Internet

It was not exactly the best of weather outside. So, Kristin Livdahl and her 10-year-old daughter were staying indoors, playing with Amazon's smart speaker, Alexa Echo, by leveraging its "challenges" feature.

You can try this with any smart speaker; wake up your smart speaker—Alexa or Google—and say, "Give me a challenge to do." You will be presented with something relatively banal, like a challenge to tie a shoe in 10 seconds or create a logo for yourself. There's little purpose to the challenges other than keeping people occupied.

So, Livdahl and her daughter passed the time accomplishing Alexa's challenges. Alexa pulled some information from a physical education teacher from a YouTube challenge. She then challenged them to lie down and roll over.

When Livdahl's daughter asked for another challenge, Alexa responded: "Here's something I found on the Web. Plug in a phone charger about halfway into a wall outlet, and then touch a penny to the exposed prongs."

When Livdahl heard this, she yelled, "No, Alexa, no!" as though the smart speaker was a rabid dog going after her child.

The problem was that just as Alexa had picked an earlier challenge from YouTube, it sourced this challenge from the Our Community Now news website. The newspaper had written about a viral TikTok trend called the "penny challenge," wherein teenagers touched a penny to exposed prongs, causing the copper in the penny to short-circuit the electrical outlet and create sparks, presumably for views and misplaced giggles at the dangerous stunt.

Ironically, the article Alexa retrieved from the site was about how *dangerous* the penny challenge was, showing burned outlets and dire warnings. The article even said, "Basically, if you see your kids hovering near a wall outlet with a penny in hand, put a stop to the prank." The source article's title, in fact, was "Watch Out, Parents—the Viral 'Outlet Challenge' Has Kids Doing the Unthinkable!" But none of this mattered for Alexa AI's system. It had missed all the warnings and negative cues from Our Community Now and doled out a lethal challenge to a 10-year-old.

After much media attention, Amazon fixed the error. For its part, Our Community Now added "Obviously, do NOT attempt this!" in parentheses in the article title. But this habit of regurgitating information from the Internet is not unique to Amazon Alexa. It is, in some sense, the industry standard.

A Twitter user posted a problematic screenshot from Google when searching for "Had Seizure, now what?" Google displayed the answer in a feature snippet at the top of its web page, designed to provide quick, convenient, and actionable results atop the regular search results. This is especially helpful when searching Google from your phone because you don't need to scroll to find the most relevant information. It's also useful when searching via smart speakers and an immediate answer is desired.

Regarding the seizure question, Google excerpted the answer from a University of Utah Health article entitled "What to do During & After a Seizure." The feature snippet atop Google's search results read: "Hold the person down or try to stop their movements. Put something in the person's mouth (this can cause tooth or jaw injuries). Administer CPR or other mouth-to-mouth breathing during the seizure. Give the person food or water until they are alert again."

But as a medical professional would attest, this is exactly what *not* to do when someone has experienced a seizure. Google had surfaced a relevant medical web page, but it had pulled the answer from the bulleted list titled "Do Not!" Since they operated on the same underlying search engine, this problem lived not just in Google but across Google Assistant and Google's smart devices when responding perilously to a life-threatening question.

The problem was fixed from multiple angles. The University of Utah deleted the bulleted list. Google no longer shows feature snippets for searches about what to do in case of seizure.

In both examples, if the requestors had gone to the source website and read the information patiently, they would have realized that the smart speakers were wrong. But we rely increasingly on AI algorithms to get information quickly and accurately. During an emergency, after we dial 911, we instinctively go to our favorite search engine to seek answers. There is no sense of calm and cool when a friend is choking—you simply trust that the answer has been vetted. And when was the last time you cross-checked Alexa's answer to your trivia question or verified if the information provided by your smart speaker is factually true?

This highlights the contradictions in our digital lives. On the one hand, we search obsessively before buying the banalest of items, spending hours reading reviews on Amazon to find the best printer or pair of shoes. We spend days consulting product review websites like WireCutter and Consumer Reports to identify the best vacuum cleaner. But, during an emergency, when an expert's information is most needed, we often rely primarily on AI algorithms, completely ignoring that algorithms have been trained by reading the Internet.

Humans have repeatedly been told not to trust everything we read on the Internet. However, we are more than willing to trust AI systems that have learned mostly ingesting Internet-assembled knowledge. We trust it enough to entertain our kids or use it during emergencies. Your wit and common sense must continue to play a role in keeping your child safe or saving a friend in need.

So far, the Internet data sourcing incidents we've discussed have been *unintentional* failure modes. These systems failed of their own accord because they happened to look in the wrong place for information. So, what if someone intentionally tried to poison the system?

Poisoning the Well

Chances are you've had a rough day if you ever email your kids and say, "I'll be coming back home, and I will talk to you and Mom, and if you're interested, I'll explain more details."

On February 1, 2011, then Corporate Vice President of Microsoft Search, Harry Shum, was wrapping up his day at work when news broke that Google had accused Microsoft Search of plagiarizing Google's search results. Microsoft's Search engine, Bing, was downright cheating by copying Google's search results, Google's team accused. And in a "we've got the receipts" moment, Google added it had irrefutable proof of Microsoft's cheating.

Mortified by the allegations, Shum ordered a deep dive into the situation. There was a whirlwind of PR, legal, and technical layers to peel. Owing to his high-profile position leading Microsoft's search engine, Shum saw the company's embarrassment as his own. *A scandal!* So, among the flurry of emails Shum dispatched to his deputies, he also emailed his son, reassuring him that he and Bing were in the right.

What came next was nothing short of dramatic. Microsoft vigorously denied the allegation. Google denied the denial. From the *Wall Street Journal* to the BBC, the story was plastered in the media and even appeared in the monologues of late-night TV hosts Jimmy Fallon and Stephen Colbert.

When Microsoft rebranded its search efforts to Bing in 2009 to capitalize on the billion-dollar ad search market, it was already behind the curve. Google dominated the market with a 60 percent market share, and Yahoo search maintained a strong second position with 20 percent. Microsoft was a distant third, but its search had begun to gain traction and was growing fast.

Google, like any competitor, kept tabs on Bing Search. In a comparative analysis, Google noticed that sometimes Bing's top results would mirror its own. Google search engineers suspected something insidious was happening in Bing and Internet Explorer's toolbars. So, in October 2010, Google devised an unprecedented sting operation against Microsoft's Bing.

Until that time, Google had never wantonly associated a search term with a specific site. Search listings were determined algorithmically, and Google took a hands-off approach. But when engineers suspected Microsoft of copying its search results, Google's leaders decided to break their cardinal rule just this once.

Google engineers hatched a plot to trace the flow of information from Google to Bing. They created fictitious and obviously random search words and associated them with specific websites in Google Search. For instance, the word *hiybbprqag* was manually associated with the Wiltern Theater in Los Angeles. Had you Googled *hiybbprqag* in October 2010, you would have been directed to the Wiltern seating arrangement. The same search in Bing would have returned no results. The poison pill was kept secret—no one outside of these Google engineers knew that *hiybbprqag* was mapped to a theater. Similarly, the random keyword *juegosdeben1ogrande* was secretly linked to a hip-hop bling store. In all, Google created 100 such "honeypot" words and lay in wait to catch Microsoft's hand in the jar—the "Bing Sting!"

In December 2010, Google corralled 20 engineers and provided them with a fresh Windows machine with Microsoft's Internet Explorer and Bing's toolbar installed with the recommended settings. Google then tasked this recruited team to use Google's search engine and look up *hiybbprqag* and the other honeypot words. These engineers routinely did this from their homes as the Bing toolbar watched. The Bing Search engine returned empty results.

But, on New Year's Eve 2010, the Bing search engine began returning results for *hiybbprqag* and nine other honeypot words. Google concluded that the Bing toolbar had been gathering data on users as they visited the Google site and used it to improve Bing's search results. This was the smoking gun, Google concluded.

Google did not mince words when the details were revealed in February 2011. Microsoft cheated, they said. "I've got no problem with a competitor developing an innovative algorithm. But copying is not innovation, in my book," said Amit Singhal, then head of Google Search.

Was this a case of highway robbery or mistaken identity? It turns out that among the many signals Bing used to rank websites was the information that the Bing toolbar collected when a user visited a page. Called a *clickstream*, when a user clicks a new link, Bing informs Microsoft that the new page should be regarded as similar to the previous page viewed by the Internet surfer. Thus, a user's clickstream navigating from page 1, to page 2, to page 3, and so on, would be used as input to refine future searches. In the Bing Sting, Google engineers had inadvertently populated a clickstream using the search engine result for *hiybbprqag*, visiting the Wiltern theatre page after unsuccessfully searching for the fictitious term. With this tenuous association, the clickstream would eventually create a connective link for Bing to consider in subsequent searches. Because of the exceptional rarity or uniqueness of terms like *hiybbprqag*, such clickstreams instantly became blinding signals to Bing about that word appearing on the page, Google or not. Bing had memorized that relationship seen only a few times during the Bing Sting! (In fact, this behavior of the Bing toolbar had been part of Bing's software as an opt-out service since 2009. In retrospect, Google need not have conducted a covert operation to discover it.)

Ironically, Google itself fell prey to the very same tactics it had employed in the Bing Sting.

When rapper Desiigner (yes, that's Designer with an extra *i*) dropped his "Panda" single in 2016, a software engineer from lyric aggregator site Genius noted something was off. Because the rapper sings the song at a hard-to-understand pace and tone, most lyrics websites were understandably incorrect—except Google. Had you searched for the lyrics in Google at that time, an error-free version would pop up in the feature snippet right at the top. Genius suspected that Google was lifting the lyrics from the site because Genius was the only website that the author had given the authoritative lyrics. Genius did not provide the lyrics to appear in the featured snippet.

Google had outsourced lyric gathering to another company called, LyricFind. And LyricFind categorically denied that it did not scrape lyrics from Genius. So, how did lyrics from Genius end up in Google if Genius did not provide it to Google?

To get to the bottom of this mystery, Genius deployed a neat trick. The company modified the expression of apostrophes in hundreds of its lyrics—some rendered as straight apostrophes and others as curly. Lo and behold, Google showed the exact pattern of the apostrophes in its search results. To punctuate the finding, the combination of straight and curly apostrophes, when interpreted as dots and dash in Morse code, read "REDHANDED." Genius was hinting that Google had been caught red-handed for lifting lyrics from its site. From the Bing Sting, the proverbial table had turned.

When covered by the *Wall Street Journal*, Google stopped surfacing the Morse code–laced lyrics. But the second round of watermarking—this time using spaces instead of apostrophes to spell "Genius" in Morse code—caught Google again. Genius would later sue Google for copyright infringement, and LyricFind would later concede that it had unknowingly used Genius as a source for a few of its lyrics. But the case would be dismissed on a legal technicality that Genius was only a lyric aggregator and did not really own the copyright to the original lyrics.

The Bing Sting and the Genius incidents involve a form of *digital watermarking*. Like the watermarks used in currency that appear only in certain lighting conditions to discourage counterfeiting, digital watermarks can help authors claim original ownership of digital replicas of images, media, or audio.

But tampering with a dataset can also be used for nefarious purposes. Poisoning is a deliberate attempt to influence the outcome of an AI system. Just as a poisoned well affects anyone who drinks from it, poisoning the input data can corrupt the entire ML system.

There are three lessons about poisoning we can learn from these incidents.

The first lesson: modern-day machine learning systems that rely heavily on crowd-sourced Internet data are susceptible to intentional poisoning. A prime example is Wikipedia. A bored Chinese housewife spent years fabricating medieval Russian history, writing more than 200 Wikipedia articles, including made-up maps, sieges, and mines. The articles were so highly cited that Wikipedia even featured them on its web page. An AI system trained on this hallucinated data will likely regurgitate these made-up answers. In 2018, Google reported that the most advanced spammer groups attempted to throw off the Gmail spam filter by reporting massive amounts of spam emails as not spam. Because the Gmail filter learns spam/not spam in part by the labels provided by its users—be they legitimate or fake accounts—spammers conditioned filters to prepare for their own spam campaigns.

The second takeaway: poisoning attacks give an adversary the ability to fly under the radar. And in some cases, that is beneficial to the consumer. (Remember, we use the word *adversary* for anyone who violates the system's underlying assumptions.) For instance, a related trick can be used to help users escape the watchful eye of online ad agencies. Coined as *obfuscation* by Helen Nissenbaum, professor at Cornell Tech, this trick involves "the deliberate addition of ambiguous, confusing, or misleading information to interfere with surveillance and data collection."

Remember the recorded message "Calls may be recorded for quality and training purposes" when phoning a customer service helpline? When surfing the Internet, every activity is recorded and used to track your activity to serve better ads. Adversaries can hijack this feedback pathway for poisoning. These ad-tracking algorithms are more than a nuisance; it is sanctioned surveillance.

Mozilla weaponized this tracking activity to help customers cloak their activity in the interweb. Essentially, Mozilla poisoned the ad-tracking algorithms for its customers by polluting the data. It built a system called Track THIS where one can choose to appear on the Internet as a social media influencer, a doomsday prepper, a "hypebeast" interested in exclusive shoes and streetwear, or someone who is "filthy rich." For instance, when a user surfs under the "filthy rich" persona, the tool opens 100 tabs in your web browser that cater to the wealthy: sites like YSL (luxury clothing), Lancome (luxury makeup), Rolex (luxury watch), Hakkasan (high-end restaurant), and Piaget (luxury car). And just like that, your ads become instantly tailored to someone truly living the high-roller life—for a brief period until the ad trackers adapt to your middleclass Internet-surfing behavior, you can enjoy the ads intended for the uber-wealthy!

Obfuscation via poisoning has been recycled in other places. Want to trick Facebook's algorithm into thinking you are emotionally balanced? Whenever you "like" a post, the web browser extension GoRando randomly chooses the post's emotion. Worried about your privacy when an app asks to access your contacts in your phonebook? A tool called Fake Contacts 2 will literally create hundreds of fake contacts with fake numbers and names in your phone. On a similar note, to escape Instagram's prying eyes, a group of teenagers once used shared accounts to generate group behavior that hides the behavior of specific individuals. But the effects of obfuscation do not last long. Just as the effect of the magical Felix Felicis potion is temporary, so are the effects of obfuscation since modern ML systems continually learn and aggregate signals from different places.

The third lesson here is that it does not take much to poison a machine learning system, both in terms of the number of people or data points. Temporarily poisoning the ad-tracking system requires only one person—you. It took only 20 people clicking links for less than 2 weeks for Bing to incorporate the "honeypot" result. Compare this to the 400,000 volunteers in Ukraine's cyber army against Russia, which outnumbers their physical army by 2:1. Victor Zhora, deputy chief of Ukraine's information protection service, said that the cyber army is doing "everything possible to protect our land in cyberspace, our networks, and to make the aggressor (Russia) feel uncomfortable with their actions." Or consider the 50,000 that comprise China's cyber army, which Nicole Perlroth from the *New York Times* reports as constituting "an elite satellite network of contractors at front companies and universities that work at the direction of China's Ministry of State Security." Any cyber army can easily launch a campaign to poison an AI system, which could spell its knell.

The amount of data required to poison an AI system is also low. Researchers have found that by polluting examples that total just 0.1 percent of the dataset size, one can manipulate an ML model trained on the poisoned dataset. Whole systems exhibit similar susceptibility. One strong signal from those "honeypot" words from roughly 20 Google engineers was sufficient to confuse the entire Bing system. Genius only had to corrupt 100 song lyrics to capture Google's reliance on its data.

This combination of low human effort and the low number of samples is particularly good for "sting" operations. In 2010, the Russian antivirus company Kaspersky publicly complained that competitors copied outcomes they posted on the crowd-sourcing antivirus website VirusTotal. To illustrate the point, Kaspersky engineers uploaded 20 benign files but marked them as malicious. In less than 2 weeks, the files were marked as malicious by at least 14 other security firms on the same website. The crowd-sourcing site is a vulnerability vector for poisoning with little effort and only a few examples.

Today adversarial machine learning researchers have taken the number of samples required to poison to the extreme: corrupting the entire AI system with just one data point. A Stanford researchers' stunning experiment showed that even a single data point during training time could have detrimental effects on the entire ML system. In a dog vs. fish image classifier, poisoning a single dog image and labeling it as a fish in the training dataset eventually led the classifier to ascertain other dog images to be mislabeled as fish (see Figure 4-2).

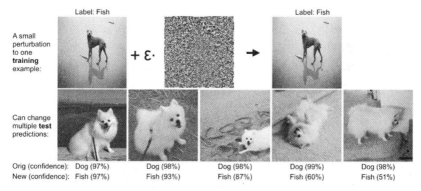

Figure 4.2   Poisoning a single training example leads to multiple failures during test time. Pang Wei Koh and Percy Liang. "Understanding black-box predictions via influence functions." International Conference on Machine Learning, 2017

Interestingly, the authors of this study corrupted the training image of the dog using adversarial examples. And it turns out there is a close connection between these two attacks.

The Higher You Climb, the Harder You Fall

Alina Oprea may very well be the doyenne of AI deception. Gilded with early signs of excellence—a podium finish at the notoriously difficult Romanian National Math Olympiad, a PhD from Carnegie Mellon University, and listed in MIT's 35 Under 35—Oprea is currently a professor at Northeastern University. There, situated in what the Boston Society of Architects dubbed one of the most beautiful buildings in the city, Oprea and her lab systematically push the boundaries for poisoning attacks against AI systems.

Are some kinds of AI systems more susceptible to poisoning than others? To answer this, Oprea teamed up with Battista Biggio, who we previously saw as an early adversarial machine learning pioneer. Together, their labs shed light on what kind of algorithms are susceptible to poisoning and adversarial examples. It was the first work of its kind, bringing together these two important attacks on AI systems.

First, they showed that just as adversarial examples transfer, poisoning attacks also transfer across different ML model types. Theoretically, this means if an adversary discovers an effective poison pill for the conversation algorithm used by Alexa, chances are, Google Assistant would also be poisoned by it, even it if used completely different ML architectures to recognize speech. The vulnerability extends across multiple platforms. There may be no "poison-proof" ML. And an attacker may be able to reuse malicious data points across models—a very powerful attacker advantage!

Second, Oprea and Biggio's joint work also pointed to another nonintuitive phenomenon. They discovered that the more complex an algorithm is, the more vulnerable it is to both poisoning and adversarial examples. This was machine learning's version of the proverb, "The higher you are, the harder you fall." A vulnerable data supply chain compounds the deployment complexity of AI systems. As a result, many organizations caution against the unnecessary development of AI. Speaking more to complexity and expectations than poisoning, Google writes in their style guide for machine learning engineers: "Rule #1: Don't be afraid to launch a product without machine learning. Machine learning is cool, but it requires data. Theoretically, you can take data from a different problem and then tweak the model for a new product, but this will likely underperform basic heuristics. If you think machine learning will give you a 100 percent boost, then a heuristic will get you 50 percent of the way there." In other words, don't discount the role of simple human ingenuity in solving a complex problem.

Yes, adversarial examples tend to be the most entertaining—who does not want to see a state-of-the-art self-driving car fumble with stickers on stop signs? But poisoning attacks are alarming—it is what keeps executives up at night. Poisoning attacks go for the AI system's proverbial artery: right to the data source itself.

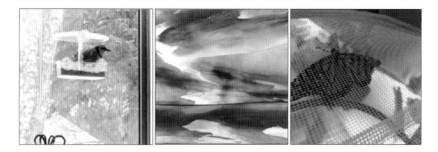

Figure 2.1 Without overthinking, what do you see in these images? If you guessed a bird, a painting, and a butterfly, then congratulations! You are 100 percent human!
COURTESY OF DAN HENDRYKS

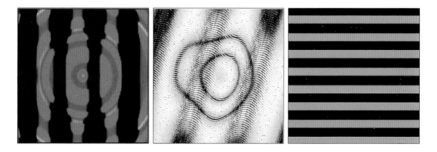

Figure 2.2 When you look at Figure 2.2, ideally you do not see a king penguin, a green snake, and a school bus.
COURTESY OF ANN NGUYEN

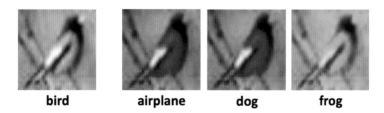

Figure 2.9 Changing the hue and saturation of an image can change how AI algorithms perceive it.
COURTESY OF HOSSEIN HOSSEINI

Figure 2.10 The boxes show how the AI algorithm recognizes the objects. When a random polar bar is added to the picture, the AI system gets confused—and misrecognizes the entire image.
COURTESY OF AMIR ROSENFELD

Figure 3.2 An adversarial T-shirt in a controlled setting means that AI may not recognize the person wearing it.
COURTESY OF ZUXUAN WU

One of Evtimov's stop signs with stickers that confuse AI vision, on display at London's Science Museum.
SOURCE: Twitter/Earlence Fernandes

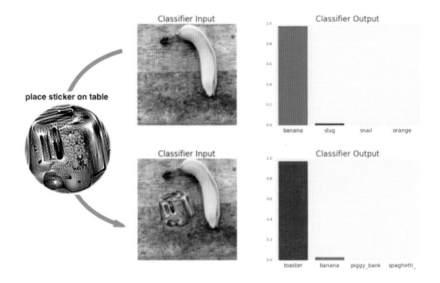

Figure 3.8 Adversarial noise can be printed on a physical patch to confuse AI systems.

COURTESY OF TOM B. BROWN AND DANDELION MANÉ

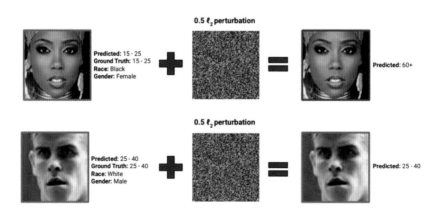

Figure 6.2 Researchers found that a Black female face is more susceptible to adversarial noise than a white male face.

COURTESY OF VEDANT NANDA

Chapter 5

Can You Keep a Secret?

This is an excerpt of a conversation between popular podcaster Lex Fridman and Elon Musk, CEO of Tesla, in 2019:

Lex Fridman:	*Recently, there are a few hackers who tricked the autopilot to act in unexpected ways—adversarial examples. So, we all know that neural network systems are very sensitive to minor disturbances to these adversarial examples on input. Do you think it's possible to defend against something like this?*
Elon Musk:	*So, yeah.*
Lex Fridman:	*. . . for long for the industry?*

(Elon Musk heard laughing)

Lex Fridman:	*Can you elaborate on the confidence behind that answer?*
Elon Musk:	*Well, you know, a neural net is just like a bunch of matrix math. You have to be like a very sophisticated somebody who really has neural nets and like basically reverse engineer how the matrix is being built and then create a little thing that's just exactly what causes the matrix math to be slightly off.*

But it's very easy to block that by having basically, anti-negative
recognition. It's like if the system sees something that looks like a
Matrix hack, exclude it.
This is such an easy thing to do.

Musk may be right when it comes to SpaceX and Starlink, but
when it comes to the supposed ease of defending against adversarial examples, he is quite mistaken.

If there is one thing machine learning experts unequivocally
agree on, it is that defending and detecting adversarial examples
is hard. It's so hard that Ian Goodfellow—the very researcher who
coined the term *adversarial examples* and who has made path-
breaking contributions to securing AI systems—stopped working on them.

"I hit a wall when trying to come up with a solution," Goodfellow told us over a Zoom call. After working on them for 5 years
straight, he gave up on adversarial machine learning in 2016 and
diverted his mental energy to other areas of AI research. But why?
Why is defending against adversarial attacks so hard? And what lessons can we learn as we secure AI systems?

Why Is Defending Against Adversarial Attacks Hard?

Ethan Burris, management professor at the University of Texas
at Austin, wrote in *Harvard Business Review* that there are two
kinds of managers. One type tends to think high level, taking a
"systems approach." They look to the future, have their heads in
the clouds, and are playing to win. He called these kinds of people
"promotion-focused" because they are quite literally promoting the
future of their organizations. The second type is managers who are
"prevention-focused." They are deep in the weeds, vigilantly thinking about the present, fighting many fires, grounded in the nitty-
gritty, and are just playing not to lose.

This framing also coarsely applies to attackers and defenders.
One can think of attackers as high-level, systems-thinking, and
promotion-focused managers. Initially, attackers needn't know

much about the ML system they are attacking to be successful. (Although they often come away with a clearer understanding of many details of the target than those who built it!) In the case of black-box attacks against ML, they needn't have detailed knowledge of the ML model they plan to attack. Still, they can be successful.

We have used the terms *adversary* and *attacker* in this book to expansively mean anyone who challenges the operating assumptions on which AI is built. For example, an adversary can be Reddit users who knew little about the inner workings of Microsoft Tay and yet were able to poison it or scholars who compose sophisticated attacks to advance AI security. What they share is a purposeful mindset. They are persistent. They might be patient. By doggedly pursuing their objectives, they "play to win."

On the other hand, because defenders must manage many risks and potential threats, their best bet is to play not to lose. For a defender to be successful, they must perceive and ward off *all threats*. This makes their position challenging. Defenders must anticipate attacks and proactively build defenses against all potential threats to their business. Defenders have a prevention-focused mindset—engaged in the details of the present—and fight many fires.

To complicate matters, attackers also have first movers' advantage in attacking AI systems. The entire field of adversarial ML started not with the question "How can we protect AI systems?" but with a statement: "Breaking this AI spam filter is interesting." Since defenders play not to lose, the moves they make are not always the most optimal, but moves that minimize the worst possible outcome from the attacker. This makes sense: when you don't know what's going to happen, preparing for the worst-case scenario helps. Because defenders cannot anticipate an attacker's moves, they play it safe by taking away the big play.

In a game of chess, both players are on the same footing. That is, each player has the same view of the board—where each piece is exactly located—and can clearly see every move the other player is making. In this setting, information is said to be symmetrical. However, in cybersecurity, the proverbial information table is tilted in favor of the adversary. Called *information asymmetry*, adversaries have an advantage because they tend to know more about the system. Why? Rob Joyce, director of cybersecurity at NSA, attributed the attacker's upper hand to their careful study of the system they plan to attack. "Attackers put in the time to know the network and the devices better than the defenders," Joyce said in a tweet. Defenders know what system they *tried* to set up, but attackers know what system was *actually* set up.

Information asymmetry is particularly exacerbated in the case of AI systems. First, one need not be a specialist to attack AI systems. From trial and error, trolls from the Internet observed that Microsoft's Tay bot was learning from their tweets and exploited that. Merely interacting with an AI system may be sufficient for the adversary. Because most AI systems are not architected with security in mind, there is virtually no security monitoring that could warn you an AI system is being tampered with. Defenders are flying dark. Finally, much of what an attacker needs to know about an AI system may already be out in the open. Called open-source intelligence (OSINT), any of this trove's publicly available resources—product blogs, marketing materials, code repositories, and academic publications—might not reveal much individually, but taken together, they provide valuable clues for adversaries.

The information asymmetry between attackers and defenders is not a phenomenon unique to AI. It is a fundamental issue in cybersecurity. But AI introduces complexities that make security even more difficult than its traditional cybersecurity counterpart.

With traditional cybersecurity, attackers target coding errors in code written by humans. That code can be analyzed, and the offending lines of software corrected or replaced—which is the reason for the regular security updates and software patches you receive on your laptop and phone. But ML models are not written explicitly by humans—an algorithm sets their parameters and weights to optimize the learning objective (for example, prediction). A careful inspection of the model parameters cannot easily reveal their vulnerabilities. And even if model vulnerabilities are discovered, there are no tools to correct them surgically. Where a software engineer can use a scalpel to change a few lines of code, today's machine learning engineer can't force a model to *unlearn* a back door or poison vulnerability. In essence, AI's bugs can't be patched.

To make matters worse, AI defenders must worry about the *universality* of AI vulnerabilities. In traditional cybersecurity, attackers often target a specific vulnerability in dated and unpatched software. Thanks to software updates, certain vulnerabilities that exist for one software version might no longer be exploited when the patch is applied. But, owing to the *transferability* property in Chapter 3, in which an adversarial example for model A is also very likely to work for model B, AI defenders cannot hide behind a particular implementation or model version. Related models *share* vulnerabilities! So, in an exacerbation of adversarial asymmetry, attackers needn't even guess your ML model version. So, the odds are stacked against defenders, especially when it comes to AI.

How do defenders fix this information asymmetry? One strategy began as a decade-long obsession with keeping AI systems under wraps: corporate researchers attempting to obfuscate the minutiae of the models or even keep entire AI systems a secret. This could be, assuming positive intent and kindly interpreting what Musk hinted at when he said you first need access to the neural nets. Corporate researchers thought locking down the aspects of the system was a remedy for keeping adversaries in the dark, preventing easy attacks.

But the opposite has happened. As we will see in the chapter, the time to topple the AI system has not decreased. Keeping things hidden is not a reliable strategy for one simple reason: like nature, adversaries will always find a way.

Masking Is Important

Recall that the attacker's goal in adversarial examples is to provide a carefully constructed input to the ML model, which might not confuse a human but will most definitely confuse the ML system to provide the wrong output. The canonical example here is how an adversary can change the pixels in an image of a panda so it still looks like a panda to us, but a state-of-the-art ML system would misrecognize it as a gibbon.

While adversarial evasion attacks affect a machine learning model's integrity, other attacks can still affect the confidentiality of the model or data. As discussed briefly in Chapter 3, *model stealing* (or *model extraction*) attacks are used by adversaries to steal the functionality of a model. The idea behind this attack is simple— prompt the model with inputs, record the outputs with the newly collected training set, and create a model that aims to mimic the victim model exactly.

More sophisticated attacks exist that use a trained model as a proxy to attack the confidentiality of the dataset it was trained on. How? Because a model is, in some sense, a summary of its training data, attacks against a model can be crafted to actually attack its training set. A *model inversion* attack attempts to approximately reconstruct private training data (such as an image of an individual's face) by observing the properties of the model's output. A *membership inference* attack aims to infer properties of the private data by observing the model's relative confidence about samples in its training set compared to other samples.

These powerful black-box attacks exploit the properties of a trained and deployed ML model, even after it has long been separated from its training set. How exactly are these black-box attacks possible?

When provided an image, most real-world machine learning systems would output two pieces of information—the decision of the image (panda or gibbon) and the ML system's corresponding confidence in its decision. Suppose you were to send an untampered image of a panda to a panda/gibbon classifier for identification. We could expect from the ML system an answer along the lines of the decision ("panda") and confidence ("100%").

In a black-box evasion threat scenario, the adversary exploits an ML system very much how a legitimate user would use the system— send an image to the ML system and observe the confidence score. The adversary's first attempt might not fool the classifier yet. (The image might still be recognized as a panda with the confidence level being "panda—99.8 percent confident; gibbon—0.2 percent confident"). But this attempt gives the adversary key information.

The changes made to the picture tipped the scale toward a gibbon, providing the attacker with a sense of direction! This feedback can then be used to modify the original image slightly differently, after which the adversary can check the progress by querying the model. The entire process is repeated until the perturbed image of the panda receives an overwhelming gibbon score of greater than 50 percent. The time to get from 0.1 percent gibbon and 50 percent gibbon might seem insurmountable, but in real-world applications, if the direction information is readily accessible, finding adversarial examples takes just seconds to complete.

The vital direction information revealed by the confidence measure of ML systems is key for how adversaries attack AI systems. Once adversaries have this key information, the exact recipe to wiggle and jiggle the tweaks until the adversary succeeds is based on gradient descent, which we learned about in Chapter 4.

To respond to the growing threats of adversarial examples, AI researchers have concocted schemes to hide the gradient information from attackers, a philosophy Papernot coined as "gradient masking" in his breakthrough work on black-box attacks on ML systems we saw in Chapter 3. The rationale is simple: mask the gradient information from malicious attackers so they can no longer use the gradient descent algorithm to synthesize adversarial examples that would fool the machine learning system. Defenders have created many innovative ways to obfuscate gradients from adversaries:

One line of thought was to completely hide confidence scores from users and provide only "hard" labels. Instead of outputting "panda—99.9 percent confident; gibbon—0.1 percent confident," the model is compelled only to report that the image is that of a "panda," dropping the confidence scores. So, any sense of progress resulting from observing "panda—99.8 percent; gibbon—0.2 percent" is kept private.

Another bucket of effort came to be called *stochastic gradients*, which aim to lead the attacker astray. Stochastic comes from the ancient Greek word *stókhos* (στόχος), denoting brick pillars. In ancient Greece, archers practiced their bow and arrow skills by haphazardly aiming at these pillars, and thus, stókhos also evolved to mean "guessing or random." So, in stochastic gradients, the defenders try to frustrate the adversary by intentionally changing the input or the output in a way that gives correct answers in bulk but provides an incomplete picture to an adversary for any one query. Receiving stochastic gradients might force the attacker to construct an attack haphazardly.

Yet a third approach aims to mislead an attacker by directly building in unreliable gradient computation into the model. "Shattered gradients" deliberately introduce instabilities into a model so that even if an attacker can estimate the gradient direction reliably, they are led down unfruitful paths. The model's output is meaningful, but the gradient direction is misleading. Alas, this provides only a limited measure of protection to a model for white-box evasion attacks.

But researchers have taken this approach even further. Rather than hide or *passively* yield misleading outputs or gradients by virtue of how the model is constructed, some have proposed *active* deception techniques to frustrate attackers and lead them down wandering paths. Aimed primarily at preventing model theft described in Chapter 3, where the attacker can copy a model by interacting with it, these approaches deliberately modify their output predictions in a way that tries to disrupt an attacker's objective. But, if the model produces deceptive outputs to an attacker, would it not also be disruptive to an ordinary user? After all, the model doesn't typically know *who* is querying it. Therein lies the genius of *active measures*. The model's output confidence (such as ostrich, 75 percent) is modified in a way that has a relatively small impact on users (such as ostrich, 55 percent), but for an attacker who needs thousands of queries for a black-box attack, the carefully crafted and accumulated error is precisely designed to lead them astray. The model they steal does not replicate the target model!

Regardless of the particular approach, the defenders' ultimate motive is to limit what an adversary can learn by probing a model. Frustrating to an attacker? Perhaps. Disincentivizing attacks by making them more costly or intensive? Hopefully!

But as the inscription on the gates of Hell in *Dante's Inferno*'s third canto tells us, which translates to "Abandon all hope, ye who enter."

Because It Is Possible

The js13kGames ("JS 13 K Games") is an annual programming challenge that, at first blush, sounds jejune: create a real-time strategy video game using a popular programming language. But there is a catch: your program should be less than 13 kilobytes, meaning you will have to design an entirely playable video game with graphics, storyline, and content in less space than it takes to store a simple Word document on your computer. This is a challenge of not just creativity but creativity in constraints.

Most people who enter this challenge are game designers, but Nicholas Carlini is not most people. Carlini is one of the most respected adversarial ML researchers who has a doctoral degree from UC Berkeley and a plum job with Google but no credentials in game design. If you were to ask Carlini why he entered this competition (and was a podium finisher in 2020), he would laugh and say, "I like random things."

The road to one of the most competitive computer science schools was anything but obvious for Carlini. He was not a straight-A student in high school. "My grades were quite bad," he said. But there was one thing Carlini was really, really good at: programming. In fact, he was good enough that his Sequoia High School principal recruited him to build the school's website, which helped him land a respectable recommendation letter.

You can see Carlini's zest for programming on his website, nicolas.carlini.com. The entire site is a wunderkammer, a coder's cabinet of curiosities, peppered with steps to emulate the world's first commercially produced and highly outdated microprocessor, Intel 4004, on top of John Conway's *Game of Life*, which Carlini has been working on for the last 10 years. There's the recipe for building your own 3D shadow rendering engine in JavaScript. It's all very niche, interesting, and perhaps of little general value. Carlini's creative projects are delightfully obscure, tied together by the underlying theme of "because it is possible."

But, for someone who builds a lot of things, Carlini's GitHub profile succinctly states, "I break things." As a teenager, Carlini crashed the library system by scanning random barcodes in the return section. During a routine dental checkup as a high school student, as he was waiting for a dental checkup, he poked around and found out that his doctor's office databases were riddled with security bugs. At Berkely, he formalized his hacking knowledge thanks to highly respected cybersecurity expert Professor David Wagner's network security class.

Wagner, himself, has a wonderful eye when it comes to hacking. In an email to a group of "cyberphunks" (a play on the word *cyberpunks*), Wagner and his officemate, Ian Goldberg, both first-year PhD students at Berkeley, announced they found security bugs in the then wildly popular Netscape browser. "Happy Hacking," the message ended. The impact? "Software Security Flaw Puts Shoppers on Internet at Risk" the news read on the front page of the *New York Times* two days later, on September 19, 1995.

Fast-forward almost two decades later, and things would come full circle. Carlini was smitten by Wagner's elan and éclat for finding vulnerabilities in software—so much so that Carlini stayed on at Berkeley for a PhD program and continued breaking random things, from operating systems to Chrome browsers. Armed with this knowledge, he raked in "bug bounties"—money awarded to hackers when security vulnerabilities were reported—from everywhere from Yahoo to PayPal. Eventually, Carlini felt the need to knuckle down and find a cohesive topic for his dissertation. His choice? Wearable devices, their AI, and how to attack them. But as all doctoral students would attest, the scope of his work intensified, eventually becoming AI and how to attack it.

As the most well-studied of all the attacks on machine learning systems, adversarial examples are a great testbed for understanding the complexity of algorithms. Since 2016, researchers have published almost two papers a day on this topic. Adversarial examples are, in some sense, the eye of this adversarial ML research storm. Novel attacks and defenses continue to be published at a breakneck speed.

If so many researchers are racing to look into the area, clearly our knowledge of securing AI systems from such adversarial manipulation must also be advancing at a rapid pace, right? Unfortunately, no. MIT Professor Aleksander Madry, noted adversarial ML expert, points out in his lecture notes, that the succession of attacks and defenses is still "a cottage industry," adding that "time and time again, these defenses have been repeatedly broken, often extremely quickly."

Carlini shines not just because he breaks machine learning systems, but he does it with an unmistakable sense of sprezzatura. "I get the feeling that people vastly over-estimate the difficulty of breaking published defenses," Carlini concluded after doing a live recording of him breaking a state-of-the-art defense against adversarial machine learning. In one published work that broke a different defense that he titled "Is AMI (Attacks Meet Interpretability) Robust to Adversarial Examples?" he summarized his findings in the abstract in a single word: "no."

But there was a seminal moment in 2018 that drove this point home. Many ML researchers had bookmarked January 29, 2018, on their calendars because that was when the prestigious conference International Conference on Learning Representations (ICLR for short and pronounced "eye-clear") would announce whether their work had been selected to be presented at the venue. It was the same conference where the existence of adversarial examples by Szegedy and collaborators had been announced four years prior. Presenting at this venue would certainly burnish one's credentials as a bona fide ML researcher. When the announcements went out on January 29, 2018, they unsurprisingly included defenses to adversarial examples from top brass universities—including Stanford, Berkeley, Carnegie Mellon University, and others.

But just three days after the announcement, Anish Athalye, in collaboration with Carlini and Wagner, put up a website showing how seven of nine defenses just announced at this prestigious ICLR conference had been broken.

The problem is not that defenses are imperfect—that is to be expected, because nature always finds a way—but it *continues* to happen. First, in 2017, Papernot, while working on transferability and black-box attacks, showed that a slew of defenses using gradient masking had been broken. Next, in 2018, Athalye and Carlini broke seven of nine defenses. And then, in 2020, almost two years to the date later, Carlini would once again break 13 defenses.

You would have thought that researchers would have learned in 2017, but to see this problem rear its head again in 2018 and then again in 2020 almost makes you stop and ask: is the field just going in circles? What's so hard about building defenses for ML systems?

Masking Alone Is Not Good Enough

Battista Biggio, one of the adversarial ML elders, was not too surprised when news of Carlini's 2018 ICLR-defenses-breaking hijinks of breaking was published. He later told *Wired* magazine, "The machine learning community is lacking a methodological approach to evaluate security."

The common culprit connecting these events from 2017 through 2020? Gradient masking. Defenders had been trying to naively obfuscate gradient information and keep it a secret from adversaries, but each of these would prove insufficient for a bulletproof defense.

For instance, as previously discussed, researchers tried to use hard labels containing no confidence information, hoping to make it onerous for adversaries to construct adversarial examples using gradient descent. However, researchers like Papernot and Carlini showed that adversaries could reconstruct gradients by simply interacting with the system. How? Essentially, an adversary would first build a surrogate ML model using the responses from the target model. This surrogate model is controlled by the attacker, emitting both labels and confidence. Then, the attacker can leverage the simplest and most effective white-box attacks, leading to adversarial examples that work against the surrogate model. Then, by the property of transferability, the adversary could use these examples to bypass the victim model.

Earlier, we saw how black-box attacks helped with constructing a "bargain bin model" to find adversarial examples. Turns out this recipe of "copying, evading, and then transferring an attack" was more sinister still! It is impervious to masking. The method by which you fortify your model from adversarial examples—stochastic gradients or gradient shattering—ultimately would not matter. Black-box attacks help adversaries achieve their goals. That's another blow to defenders.

Clearly, our attempts to secure the algorithm by keeping specific artifacts about the algorithm a secret have not proven useful, though there is another alternative.

So far, we have been thinking about the problem from an algorithm and its minutiae level. How about we go up a level to make the entire system a secret? If you cannot hide the individual chickens from the wolves, why not conceal the entire coop?

An Average Concerned Citizen

January is a busy month for many, but it can get extra busy if you are working in consumer electronics. Held in Las Vegas at the beginning of the year, the Consumer Electronic Show is the largest technology convention. In 2020, it drew more than 170,000 attendees, with the convention floor spreading across 52 football stadiums worth of space. If an electronic item had a button or connected to the Internet, it was most likely debuted at CES first. Virtually every electronic brand one can think of—Samsung, Motorola, Microsoft, and Google—queue up at CES, announcing the latest and greatest technology that year.

All brands except for one: Apple. The iconoclast since the beginning, Apple had eschewed any presence at the CES trade show and instead makes its own separate announcements.

That's why a 2019 Apple billboard ad appearing during CES in Vegas was even more conspicuous: "What happens on your iPhone stays on your iPhone," it declared. If you have ever noticed Apple ads, privacy has always been front and center, overtly reinforcing Apple's steadfast commitment to the cause and subtlety, outlining its defining differentiator. The subtext has always been, "We are not like the others. We don't let anyone else but you access your data." But upcoming events would test this claim.

On August 5, 2021, Apple announced a slew of child safety measures, and key among them was to curb the distribution of child sexual abuse material (CSAM), a catchall term for content that shows children being forced into sexually explicit activities. The entire initiative appeased even one of Congress' fiercest Big Tech critics, Senator Richard Blumenthal of New York, who, in a rare moment of praise, called the move a "welcome, innovative, and bold step."

Using a machine learning system called NeuralHash, any photo uploaded from an iPhone or iPad as it synced to iCloud was automatically scanned for child pornography matching your photo against explicit images in the national CSAM database. Well, not the images exactly.

First, images from the CSAM database are passed through the NeuralHash machine learning system, converting each image to a string of numbers called a *hash* that serves as the image's fingerprint. Apple stores this database of CSAM hashes on your device. Each time you attempt to transmit a photo from your iPhone or iPad, the NeuralHash system converts your photo to a hash. Your photo's hash is compared to the CSAM database hash stored on your device. If there is a match, Apple begins to take note. If there were more than 30 photo hash matches with the national CSAM database, Apple would review the photos manually and report your account to the National Center for Missing and Exploited Children, which in turn would involve law enforcement authorities. See Figure 5-1.

The crux of NeuralHash, as Apple noted, is to ensure that identical and visually similar images result in the same hash. (Images that are different from one another result in different hashes.)

NeuralHash: 101011...   NeuralHash: 101011... NeuralHash: 00010...

Figure 5.1   The left and center images are visually similar and hence have a similar NeuralHash, whereas the image on the right is completely different, and thus its NeuralHash is completely different.

Apple noted that the false positive rate—the chances the system would misidentify something as CSAM—was extremely low. . .to the tune of 1 in 1 *trillion* per year. To put this in perspective, Apple claims that it is 10 million times more likely that an asteroid will destroy a city than its system misidentifying a photo on your iPhone as CSAM. To further burnish the credentials of its new system, Apple roped in world-renowned cryptographers to corroborate that its protocol for flagging CSAM was secure and seal-proof.

While Apple provided a technical overview of NeuralHash, the real model was kept under wraps. Only a small clique approved by Apple had access to NeuralHash's inner workings. Even as the owner of an Apple device, you could not inspect NeuralHash or its workings to understand what was going on. That NeuralHash was on your phone was like an open secret—but a secret you weren't "in" on. The entire system was shrouded in mystery. Very Apple-esque.

Scanning images for CSAM is not new—Google, Facebook, Microsoft, and others do it as you upload your photos to their clouds. The entire national CSAM database was irreversibly encrypted on your iPhone or iPad, and the NeuralHash system ran on your end device, matching every photo you uploaded to iCloud against the database.

That's the technology. But the public and press read, "Apple is browsing my images." To the average citizen, what happened on your iPhone no longer stayed on your iPhone. There was criticism from civil liberties organizations and privacy advocates. The German parliament minced no words. It called Apple's move the "biggest breach of the dam for the confidentiality of communication that we have seen since the invention of the Internet." Everyone seemed to be upset that Apple had reneged on its privacy promises. The critics cried that Apple is scanning your phone for child pornography today, but tomorrow, Apple could kowtow to oppressive governments, surveil journalists' phones, and snoop in on conversations. The outcry came from the likes of Edward Snowden to Alex Stamos, former Facebook chief security officer, and other privacy scholars. Apple repeatedly denied this slippery slope argument and, at one point, went on full-on damage control, including a carefully orchestrated interview with executives, putting together FAQs about scanning, and releasing detailed documentation.

But no amount of PR spin could save Apple from what was to come from a cartoon face. Before August 17, 2021, the name Asuhariet Ygvar was exclusively known to readers of the niche Japanese comic "Lotte no Omocha," as the spunky, blue-eyed princess from the magical kingdom of Ygvarland. But the hitherto arcane name would light up virtually all tech news publications when a Reddit user with the AsuharietYgvar pseudonym and a matching cartoon profile picture posted in the Machine Learning community board that they had reverse-engineered the Neural-Hash model.

The user posted detailed steps for anyone to find the Neural-Hash model on their iPhone or iPad and tamper with it. The goal was to invite the 2.2 million users on the messaging board to experiment with the NeuralHash model and find issues in the algorithm before Apple widely deployed it. AsuharietYgvar signed off their post, "Happy Hacking"—a nod to the 1990s cyberpunk messaging boards that the likes of David Wagner, Carlini's advisor who is a prolific hacker himself, visited.

The messaging board members instantly upvoted the post. News that someone had reverse-engineered and shared the recipe for anyone else to do the same, soon began to spread to other messaging boards focused on computer forensics to cybersecurity to conspiracy. The cat was out of the bag.

We are using "they" to refer to AsuharietYgvar because we don't know much about the person—who they are, where they are from, or even if AsuharietYgvar is their real name. AsuharietYgvar did tell the *Register* publication that they are just "an average concerned citizen."

Until now, we only had Apple's word that NeuralHash was robust, but because the entire system was kept a secret from the public, we had no way to verify Apple's claims. But, when AsuharietYgvar reverse engineered the NeuralHash model and released it to the public to test, suddenly it democratized the testing. You didn't have to be a world-renowned cryptographer or be part of Apple's chosen clique. Anyone could now poke holes into NeuralHash and evaluate Apple's claims.

And poke they did. AsuharietYgvar showed that NeuralHash could be fooled by simply cropping an image and rotating it. Practically speaking, this means a malicious person could crop a child pornography image, and NeuralHash would not be able to match it with the image in the CSAM database. We already saw this in Chapter 2—how simple acts of cropping or rotating an image messed with AI systems used to detect skin cancer; the same also seemed to apply to Apple's NeuralHash system.

Next, Cory Cornelius, a researcher from Intel Labs, dealt another blow. Within a day of AsuharietYgvar releasing the steps to reverse engineer the model, Cornelius showed that a picture of a dog and that of a static gray background had identical NeuralHash fingerprints. This further questioned Apple's claim of NeuralHash's efficacy.

Apple tried to minimize the damages, saying that the reverse-engineered NeuralHash algorithm was a generic ML model and not the final one. Apple also pointed out that the human review process can attempt to catch these sorts of failures in NeuralHash. But it was too late. Seeing NerualHash's veracity coming into question, the chorus of the concerned reached a crescendo. Though it was announced with fanfare, Apple quietly removed all references to CSAM scanning and postponed its release to the "future."

These incidents raise a fundamental question: if researchers with a "because-it-is-possible" attitude and assumed good intentions could replicate a complex system, what can come of those with malicious intentions?

Security by Obscurity Has Limited Benefit

A key lesson from this chapter is an oft-repeated tenet of cybersecurity: "security by obscurity" ultimately provides little benefit. Adversaries, like nature, will always find a way.

More broadly, keeping AI models locked up like Kentucky Fried Chicken's secret spice may not provide the secrecy or security you think. If there is an inherent economic, political, or social value attached to your AI system, then you can assume that your AI system will eventually be attacked.

One of the common refrains we hear when we talk about attacks on AI systems is that the "model is for internal use only," and no one "outside" will be able to interact with it. Our own experience in attacking AI systems shows that this assumption is faulty—there is no such thing as "internal only." If you have an AI system in your product, you may safely assume it can be compromised regardless of the protections you imbue it with. A corollary learning is that adversaries are also users of your system.

Take Mr. Yu of No 5 Fushun Road in Qingdao City, who ordered a 2-year subscription to Norton Security Antivirus, a 2-year subscription to Symantec Endpoint Antivirus, a 2-year subscription of Kaspersky, and, finally, 2 years of McAfee. One person ordering so many antivirus products was already a red flag. Then there was the scale of the order. Mr. Yu didn't just place this order for 1 computer; he placed orders for 30 computers. And there's also the fishy fact that No 5 Fushun Road maps to the front desk of a hotel.

That's because Mr. Yu might not even be a real person. Cyber-security company Recorded Futures investigated these red flags and more to conclude that this is a front for China's People Liberation Army (PLA) unit focused on cyberattacks. There has already been a spate of Chinese state-sponsored attacks designed to find holes in commercial antivirus solutions. For instance, Google's threat analysis team found that Chinese state-sponsored attackers targeted members of President Joe Biden's campaign as part of cyber espionage by posing as McAfee and asking the victims to install the antivirus, which simultaneously downloaded malware into the system.

It should come as no surprise that adversaries are regular users of the products they intend to attack. As Recorded Futures showed in its analysis, to attack a system, adversaries first need to use the system and test how the product is defended. Perhaps this is one reason that the U.S. government took export control one step further when it became the first country to specifically prohibit the export of specific AI systems.

But laws and sanctions have never stopped attackers from trying. One can't ignore that nation-states are ably equipped with a potentially unrivaled amount of ML knowledge, computing power, and virtually any resource the attackers might need to succeed in their campaigns.

The Opportunity Is Great; the Threat Is Real; the Approach Must Be Bold

"My colleagues, every statement I make today is backed up by sources, solid sources," the speaker enunciated clearly into the microphone as the world watched on February 5, 2003. "These are not assertions. What we're giving you are facts and conclusions based on solid intelligence," he added as the CIA director, strategically placed behind him to bolster the message, looked deadpan into the camera.

The world would soon learn that this intelligence was anything but solid. Colin Powell, former Secretary of State, would later call his speech at the United Nations justifying America's invasion of Iraq "a blot" on his record. To put it mildly, America's rationale to wage war stemmed from questionable evidence; it was a $2 trillion gaffe. National security experts widely see Powell's 2003 episode as an irrecoverable blow to America's credibility in the United Nations. That is what happens when you try to convince the world with faulty intelligence.

The 9/11 attacks were a turning point in how America stitches together intelligence about its adversaries. Before that, every arm of the government collected its own intelligence: the CIA was responsible for monitoring adversaries outside America; the FBI monitored for adversaries inside America. The Navy monitors an adversary coming via the sea. The problem was that the Federal Aviation Administration (FAA), which was responsible for airport security, maintained no-fly lists that were not updated based on the intelligence collected by the CIA, FBI, Navy, or other agencies.

"Responsibility and accountability was diffuse," found the independent 9/11 Commission. If you can liken the U.S. government to a team playing (American) football, there was "no quarterback" to coordinate with other players, the commission added.

To remediate this, the U.S. government created the Office of Director of National Intelligence (or ODNI for short), which essentially helps to coordinate intelligence collected from the 17 or so agencies and compile the canonical "big picture" for decision-makers. With the need to assimilate all these data pieces and connect the dots between them, ODNI naturally turned to machine learning.

The pace of information gathered by the U.S. government far exceeds what the intelligence community can handle. From 2004 to 2005, the amount of audio backlog that had not been translated doubled. Thousands of hours of secretly recorded audio conversations of gathered intelligence from Iraq gathered dust. Robert Mueller, then FBI director who skyrocketed to public fame when he led the Special Counsel investigating President Donald Trump, testified that there just were not enough conversant Arabic speakers, and even fewer who speak in less common languages. In 2018, it was estimated that to process all the satellite images solely by hand (with no automation), the U.S. government would need to scale its intelligence team by millions of analysts.

But given how easy it is to break AI systems, what should be the guiding principles to keep AI systems safe in such a mission-critical application?

What was the ODNI's plan to secure its AI system?

The answer is no secret. In fact, you could have listened to the entire strategy had you been at Georgetown University on September 25, 2019.

Entering Gaston Hall at Georgetown University, as the *Washington Post* reported, is "like walking into the middle of an illuminated manuscript." Paneled floors, classical muses, and gilded cartouches abound in this cavernous space. This hallowed DC auditorium has hosted everyone from U.S. Supreme Court Justice Sonia Sotomayor to rapper and actor Donald Glover. It is where you bring people with prominent voices and literally put them on a stage. On September 25, 2019, Gaston Hall hosted Sue Gordon, the ODNI's then-second banana, to lay out how intelligence organizations use AI for national security. No one knows ODNI better than Gordon. After all, she gave ODNI its informal motto: "If it is knowable and it is important, then we know it."

The who's who of Washington DC filed in to hear Gordon's thoughts on how AI is shaping national security and how the ODNI is responding to it. Gordon cut right to the chase. "It's pretty cool if Netflix recommends to me the wrong film. It will not work if what the intelligence community does is get a recommendation for a target that is not sound," Gordon acknowledged. ODNI anticipated the same attempts to fool AI sensors used in intelligence collection. "Because it's not just theft of data that our adversaries would seek to influence. It will be the decisions that our machines are making," she added.

Gordon was referencing and reflecting on the ODNI's past experience. Adversaries are constantly manipulating America's capabilities to produce actionable intelligence. For instance, one of the roles of the National Geospatial-Intelligence Agency (NGA) is to provide "strategic intelligence that allows the president and national policymakers to make crucial decisions on counterterrorism, weapons of mass destruction, global political crises." And our enemies are aware of our capability. As a retired U.S. Army Colonel noted to NPR, "Most of the countries in the world know our satellite capabilities and use them to spoof us and to fool us." So, it should come as no surprise that Gordon—a former leader at the NGA—would anticipate the risks of AI system failures.

That's why in January 2019, when ODNI released its AI strategy under the title "Augmenting Intelligence Using Machines" (AIM), its call out to adversarial ML was noteworthy. "That advantage is fleeting and fragile" if the system is not built with security, safety, and reliability in mind, the report highlighted.

"The level of effort to fool an AI algorithm is considerably lower than to develop them," the report somberly mentions—a testament to the kind of adversarial hijinks we saw in Chapter 2, or the evasion of Apple's NeuralHash system by simply cropping or rotating. The report urgently made a case for the intelligence community to "be willing to rethink or abandon processes and mechanisms designed for an earlier era." Simply relying on old-school obfuscation and encryption to keep AI systems a secret will not work.

So, what is ODNI's plan to tackle these problems? "Manage uncertainty by achieving acceptable risk."

Every activity involves risk. For instance, any form of human interaction during COVID presented a risk. But we all had to go out to get groceries, pick up medication, or just take a break from our homes.

ODNI faced the reality of risk head-on. In a quote fit to print on a Hallmark card, they acknowledged that "the opportunity is great; the threat is real; the approach must be bold."

First, they acknowledged that there are adversaries out there. And they prepared for the worst-case scenario. "We have highly sophisticated adversaries with access to the same tools, their own data, and experts trained in the same universities as our own people," the report said.

As they say, the first step in fixing a problem is admitting you have one.

ODNI followed this up with a list of questions that systematically made anyone who used AI in the intelligence community to question and assess their assumptions and assess the risk of deploying the AI system. The report urges the intelligence community to ask questions like "What benefits and risks, including risks to civil liberties and privacy, might exist when this AI is in use? Who will benefit? Who or what will be at risk? What is the scale of each and the likelihood of the risks? How can those risks be minimized and the remaining risks adequately mitigated? Do the likely negative impacts outweigh likely positive impacts?"

ODNI then brought an "assume-breach" mindset to the AI engineers. The tenet is to assume that the critical system you are protecting has been tampered with and instrumented to detect anomalies. Here is how Ben Huebner, the chief of ODNI's Civil Liberties, Privacy, and Transparency Office, put it: "If we're providing intelligence to the president that is based on AI analytics, and he asks—as he does—'How do you know this?' that's a question we have to be able to answer." So, instead of focusing simply on getting things right, ODNI emphasized diagnosing what the AI system produces.

Organizations like ODNI that are proactive in securing AI systems are more the exception than the rule. But ODNI's approach to securing AI systems via a comprehensive AI risk management system is a template for how other organizations follow suit.

Gordon calls this "shared creation." As she would tell *Wired* magazine, "The government has something cool to add because we have a really particular view of the threats we face. And it will benefit us in terms of national security, but it equally benefits every aspect of American life."

This particularly resonates for adversarial machine learning, where attacks predate defenses. Since ODNI and the U.S. government face active threats to subvert AI systems, it makes sense for them to take a stab at securing AI systems. The resulting good practices that come out of this can benefit anyone securing AI systems.

Swiss Cheese

But what about Musk's idea of detecting adversarial examples? It sounds intuitive. If we devise a method to reliably detect adversarial examples, then the problem of evading AI systems using adversarial examples would be moot. When an image is presented to the AI system, it is vetted by the detection system. If the system detects it as an adversarial example, it would be rejected and not considered for input.

But Carlini, like the grim reaper with a scythe, broke 10 state-of-the-art detection systems in a seminal paper entitled "Adversarial examples are not easily detected." Carlini concluded, "Adversarial examples are much more difficult to detect than previously recognized." For someone like Carlini, who by every yardstick is measured, the line practically screams. It also helps shed light on why Goodfellow hung up his boots after a stellar run in adversarial examples. Indeed, we would like to think that normal images and adversarial examples have uniquely different properties. But Carlini's work points otherwise. At the end of the day, adversarial images are just images. Unlike oil and water, normal images and adversarial examples cannot be separated. The carefully perturbed noise added to an image to make it adversarial is more like a sugar cube in hot chai. This is the challenge in detecting adversarial examples.

Then, there is another problem. Even if researchers conceive of methods to detect adversarial examples, would they use machine learning? And if so, could those models not be evaded themselves? The general consensus is that because the composition of the detector-with-model is just another model, this can be defeated by the same probing techniques lethal to the original model. Detection approaches can temporarily delay an evasion of the protected model while the attacker is learning to evade the meta-detection model.

In a bit of adversarial irony, the one technique that reliably decreases an attacker's success rate is a sort of inoculation. In fact, Fridman remarks on this technique in the very podcast in which Musk claimed it was easy thing to do. Called *adversarial retraining,* the defender attacks their *own* model in its most exposed and vulnerable form. By collecting adversarial examples of pandas that appear as gibbons to the model, she can *retrain* the model to explicitly instruct it that these illusions are indeed pandas. Adversarial retraining is a sort of vaccine that allows the learning algorithm to fight its blind spots and take a more expansive view of what is a panda. The result? The model inherits the skepticism of having previously been deceived: it is now tricked less often but is also quite jaded about every image it encounters. Such is the cost of this particular vaccine: adversarial training can reduce the model's performance.

The conclusions in this chapter have been grim. Gradient masking doesn't work. Obfuscation techniques fail. Detections don't work. Adversarial retraining falls short. But research in adversarial defenses continues to progress. A few more techniques have likely been proposed while you were reading this book. Can they, too, be broken? Is defense actually hopeless, like Dante's description of Hell's hallway?

We needn't despair.

When COVID hit, little was known about the virus, and no vaccine was in sight, so we used a variety of tools at our disposal to stave off the pandemic: masks, hand washing, social distancing, good ventilation, and quarantining. Individually, these prevention mechanisms are not foolproof; together, they fortified us against the virus. Healthcare workers call it the "Swiss cheese model." If you liken each of the protection mechanisms to a slice of Swiss cheese and stack all of them up, it is highly unlikely you would find all the holes in the cheese slices aligning.

Security experts call this strategy of using a variety of safeguards, which individually may be fallible but together buttress the barricade against the adversary, *defense in depth*. Each layer of defense raises the cost to an attacker. It disincentivizes the attacker from attacking *your* model because there may be cheaper targets. Unfortunately, the economics of attackers and defenders is a little like that joke your uncle likes to tell: you don't have to outrun the bear; you just have to outrun the other hikers. So, every layer in your protective stack can help prevent *your* model from attack because there may be cheaper methods or easier victims.

Defense in depth is what Dawn Song, professor at UC Berkeley (who collaborated with Eykholt and Evtimov on the stop sign attack), advocated for in an another interview with Fridman when discussing adversarial examples in the context of fooling self-driving cars. It is good to have a variety of defenses and sensors to supplement ML systems in safety-critical settings, all fitly framed and layered to manage and reduce AI risk.

Having an adversarial mindset is at the crux of security. Indeed, some of the most promising technology defenses—adversarial retraining and active measures—are based on thinking like an adversary. That mindset can be up leveled. Security risk assessments for AI systems, like the one used by ODNI, are processes that allow organizations to view their systems from an attacker's perspective in a cybersecurity context. They ask what security controls should be in place for a given asset.

But who is proactively thinking like an adversary when it comes to AI? How can security risk assessments and defense in depth become the norm? What would induce an organization to adopt this process? That's the next chapter.

Chapter 6
Sailing for Adventure on the Deep Blue Sea

J ason's quest is a Panhellenic tale as old as time. Guided by Athena, the goddess of Wisdom, Jason sails on the Argo with an all-star team of 50 Greek heroes, including the likes of Hercules and Orpheus, seeking the golden fleece.

Named after the intrepid traveler, the JASON advisory group is a star-studded team of Nobel laureates, scientists, and professors that advises the U.S. Department of Defense (DoD) on strategic topics. The DoD tasks this distinguished group of experts to investigate thorny issues in national security—everything from hypersonic missiles to quantum mechanics to the U.S. census—and JASON comes back recommendations. The group typically begins meeting in the summer each year, yet it's only an amusing coincidence that JASON acronymizes July, August, September, October, and November. The entire JASON group has an aura of mystery around it: you cannot apply to be a JASON member; you are recruited into the advisory group by other JASON members. JASON members observe an impressive omertà and actively hide from the limelight, letting their work speak for itself. Like the Greek myth, there are around 50 active members in the group.

The DoD has always been interested in AI. Even from its early days, AI was destined to become a tool for geopolitical, technological, and military advantage. But after the impressive results in the ImageNet competition and the compelling victory of AlphaGo over professional player Lee Sodol in a game of Go, the DoD sought to understand how such AI systems would fare in the real world, outside of gameplay. The group was also aware of the intensified scrutiny of AI governance in recent years. For example, in 2015, the *who's who* of AI and the likes of Stephen Hawking, Jack Dorsey, and Elon Musk signed a letter decrying the use of AI in autonomous weapons for fear these systems would quickly get out of human control.

Yet, such concern had not stopped U.S. adversaries or allies from charging headlong into developing AI for military advantage. Take Israel, for instance, which has become the world's de facto leader in surveillance technology. In 2020, the *New York Times* reported that Israel used AI systems to surveil and take down an Iranian nuclear scientist to handicap Iran's nuclear program. The assassination unfurled in a spectacular sci-fi setting. First, Israel used a facial recognition system to ensure the scientist was in the car. Next, it used a remote-controlled sniper with an AI system to accurately track the moving car and surgically kill the scientist as the car rolled through an intersection on an empty stretch of road. How accurate was the shot? "His wife, sitting 25 centimeters away from him in the same car, was not injured," Iranian officials noted. This precise operation was apparently carried out thousands of miles away from Israel with no Israeli forces on the ground.

Then there is Russia. With respect to AI, while China is considering a pacing threat—with the United States and China trying to one-up each other—Russia is an assertive threat. Putin declared that the nation that leads in AI "will be ruler in the world." Russia openly used the Syrian war as an AI training ground to debut their autonomous vehicles and collect thousands of hours of drone videos, possibly to train AI systems. By one estimate, Russia already had at least 150 AI systems operating as part of its weapons systems.

So, it should come as no surprise that the DoD tapped the JASON group for their advice on how the DoD should approach AI.

The group had been instructed about adversarial machine learning from experts in the field. University of Toronto Professor Nicolas Papernot of attack transferability fame briefed the group. University of Virginia Professor David Evans, who we quoted in the first chapter on the odds of successfully attacking an AI system, also briefed them. And yes, Ian Goodfellow's famous panda/gibbon picture appeared in one of JASON's reports on this topic.

Spurred by the broad AI developments, in 2017 DoD officials posed a pointed question to JASON: "Can we verify and validate [AI systems] with [a] sufficient level of built-in security and control to ensure that these systems do what we want them to do?"

JASON's answer: "Verification and validation of AI agents is, at present, immature."

In fact, JASON noted in its findings that deep neural networks, the current backbone of AI systems, "are immature" regarding "the *ilities*," referring to the qualities good software should exhibit. In other words, when it comes to explainability, reliability, maintainability, accountability, and security, AI systems are not just *under-developed*. They are totally *undeveloped*.

Approaching a decade after JASON's findings, we are still in the same, somewhat nascent state of verification of AI agents. No one knows the risks better than former U.S. Under Secretary of Defense for Policy Michèle Flournoy. In the famous picture of Obama watching the raid that killed Osama bin Laden, Flournoy was just out of the frame, among the Pentagon's top brass. Once expected to be Biden's top pick for Secretary of Defense, no one knows the DoD better than Flournoy. So, it was particularly telling when she wrote a scathing yet honest assessment of the need to build a testing and evaluation framework for AI systems. "Failure to do so will mean falling behind," Flournoy warned.

Imagine being in the middle of a war zone in an autonomous vehicle, only for it to be confused by stickers, snow, or seagulls. Without a rigorous framework for testing and evaluation, policies tuned to the sourcing and use of AI technology, tools for evaluation, and testing standards to grade their fitness for deployment would result in a lack of confidence when the nation's finest needs AI's help the most: in a combat theater. Once identified by adversaries, these AI systems would switch from an advantage to an Achilles heel.

In retrospect, DoD's tasking of JASON and the group's subsequent recommendations were prophetic. JASON's prophecy, though, transcends the DoD. Commercial organizations also lack standards for AI testing. Shouldn't consumers of autonomous cars demand that the AI system undergo rigorous and verifiable tests? If your doctor uses an AI system for diagnosis, would you not want to know that the algorithm passes a high bar for reliability?

In this chapter, let us embark on a quest of our own. Our adventure will not involve any of Jason's arduous sailing. Instead, it will be finding answers to questions. After all, *quest* and *question* share the same Latin root, *quaerere*, which means "to seek." Instead of seeking action, we will seek information and use five questions as waypoints to chart our journey:

1. What hinders corporations that build AI products from consistently prioritizing their security?
2. What appealing incentives can help organizations care more about AI security?
3. Just because an incentive exists doesn't mean it may be adopted. So, our third question looks at what regulatory efforts are already underway to move AI security from being appealing to being adopted.
4. But the devil is in the details. Our fourth question asks, what is the gap between these incentives on paper versus practice?
5. Finally, who benefits from these incentives?

So, keep these five questions in mind as we set sail for our own armchair odyssey. Fair weather and following seas!

Why Be Securin' AI Systems So Blasted Hard? An Economics Perspective, Me Hearties!

In any list where Stephen Hawking is number 7, you clearly want to know who is at the top.

That distinction belongs to Professor Ross Anderson, who was voted by the University of Cambridge's student newspaper as the "most powerful person" in an informal survey in 2003, beating everyone from Nobel Laureates to Field Medalists and West End performers. While Anderson may not have appeared on Matt Groening's *The Simpsons* as Hawkings did, Anderson's seminal contributions to cryptography have affected everything from Internet banking to the very functioning of the Internet itself.

In 2001, Anderson had a straightforward question on his mind. "Why is Information Security Hard?" The premise seemed simple enough. Why was it, he asked, that Microsoft Windows 2000, the world's most popular operating system, had so many security bugs at the time? Clearly, Microsoft had the capital and expertise to snuff out these bugs before the OS got into the customers' hands. Why didn't Microsoft just do it?

The answer would come to Anderson while couped up in a car outside a security conference in California.

While organizers of the flagship machine learning conference, NeurIPS, where adversarial machine learning had its roots, preferred the snow, the flagship conference organizers in cybersecurity seemed to favor the sun. The IEEE Symposium on Security and Privacy was lovingly called the "Oakland conference" because the organizers defaulted to meeting at the Claremont Hotel in Oakland, California, year after year. The flyer for the security conference touted famed architect Frank Llyod Wright's endorsement that the Oakland hotel was "one of the few hotels in the world with warmth, character, and charm."

But at the May 2000 Oakland conference, Anderson's best insight would not come from meetings or academic posters but rather in a car with Hal Varian, an economics professor at Berkeley, who would later go on to be Google's chief economist. The two had always been on mailing lists together, so when Anderson flew to Berkley for the conference, he talked with Varian over dinner. In fact, they talked so much that when Varian was about to drop Anderson off at the Claremont hotel, they continued talking for an hour sitting in the car. The conversation must have been worth it, because Anderson missed the one key perk of any scientific conference: the conference drink reception.

So, what was the chat about?

The insight that spurred Anderson and Varian's impassioned conversations was that Windows bugs were not a consequence of Microsoft engineers not caring about security. Rather, it was because Microsoft was in a platform race with Apple and had to put out software as fast as it could capture customers. The reason for insecurity, they posited, had little to do with motivation, know-how, or technology. The insecurity was driven by the race to quarterly earnings statements.

Anderson's theory led to a new way of thinking about the difficulty of securing systems. That clear-eyed assessment of the economic incentives of software security made decades ago still applies to our AI security conundrum today. Corporations incentivize their engineers to jump on the AI bandwagon and to AI-enabled software that delights customers, captures interest, and provides new convenience.

So why aren't organizations solving the security problem in AI before deploying their AI-powered chatbots and autonomous cars? Insecurity may have as much to do with misaligned incentives in AI as with the lack of technical solutions to security problems.

The "winner takes all" dynamic also applies to AI development. This can be attributed to three reasons Anderson identified in the early days of commercial software and the Internet, which we depict in the context of AI systems here. Consider a hypothetical company that manufactures AI smart speakers:

- **Up-front investment:** First, producing a fully functioning AI system requires a significant up-front investment. Hiring costs alone are huge. The competition for AI talent is intense, with sky-high NFL-style salaries and a limited talent pool of experts with hands-on experience. Then, the compute costs required to train machine learning models can reach tens of millions of dollars. But once the AI system is built, it requires significantly less investment to run it within a product and add experience-improving features. In economics-speak, producing AI systems has high fixed costs but low marginal costs. For example, it could cost $10 million for staffing, data collection, and compute costs for an organization to put out its first AI-powered smart speaker with a functioning voice recognition system. But it may cost only $100,000 to add a feature that keeps track of the songs you like or simultaneously plays your favorite podcast every day. So, the company that gets to the market first will have a leg up in capturing its customers.

- **High switching costs:** Next, AI systems, in general, have high switching costs for the customer. When you buy an AI-powered smart speaker for hundreds of dollars, you spend more than just the money. You spend your precious time and effort to make the smart speaker work for you. First, you train the speaker to recognize your voice. You spend time curating your to-do list there and keeping track of your reminders. Then, you start integrating your shopping notes. You look up and save recipes. You begin setting up other connected items, such as smart lights and a smart vacuum, and setting up routines for turning on the dishwasher and lights before going to bed. If you switch to a new smart speaker from another company, you will have to shell out the money and invest all this time again. In effect, you are "locked in" to the smart speaker company.

- **Mutual benefits:** Finally, the smart speaker company should strategically release new features that keep you "locked in" and happy enough to continue using the product. As a consumer, you want more people in your network to adopt the speaker. More of your friends using smart speakers means it's easier to call each other with it and share playlists and recipes. In the same vein, businesses want you to use these devices as much as possible to justify their continued investment. They want people to spend maximum time using the smart speaker. Why? Because this is where precious data from the customers can be mined and used as feedback to improve their algorithm. This is where the magic of network effects comes into play. In other words, the organization must do more than simply win the customer. It must build a sufficient network to keep them happy to use its AI system.

The trifecta of factors—the high up-front costs, the consumer's difficulty in switching systems, and the mutual benefits of using the AI features result in an AI ecosystem with few dominant players. And those dominant players often benefit from first-mover advantage. Rarely does a second mover have the momentum to capture a locked-in customer.

Given the winner-take-all dynamics in AI systems, it is only natural that organizations spend time chasing customers and not securing their AI systems. To echo what Anderson said in his 2001 work, this leads to the "we'll ship it (the product) on Tuesday and get it right by version 3" behavior. Anderson spells out that this punting of security is not because of "personal moral failing (of company leadership)" but instead is "perfectly rational behavior in many markets where network economics apply." Indeed, the current market economics of AI systems largely reward putting out a product first; it does not reward putting out a vulnerability-free product. We largely have market economics to blame for this. Anderson concluded that the insecure status quo would prevail when securing the Internet without significant nudges from an outside entity.

Anderson's conclusion addresses the first question in our quest, "Why are organizations not prioritizing securing AI systems?" Few visionary companies—mostly large AI corporations—proactively choose to secure their AI systems. These few are swimming toward a safer shore but largely against today's economic currents. For the most part, organically, the market may not "sort out" the solution on its own because organizations are too bogged down in building features and too focused on winning the market.

This eases us to the second leg of our quest (or questions!): is there a way to relieve that downward current that pushes companies to release insecure AI models? Are there external incentives that can counteract the macroeconomics? What sort of gentle prodding or nudging could make organizations care more about AI security?

Tis a Sign, Me Mateys

If you are in the United States or Canada, put down this book and look at the underside of your toaster, the side of your microwave, or any electrical appliance in your kitchen. You will find a UL sticker—which stands for Underwriters Laboratories, an independent third party that's been around for more than a century—attesting that your kitchen appliance does not spontaneously combust.

Now, if you are in Europe, the markings on your kitchen items may be a little different. Instead of a UL, you may need to look for CE (which stands for "conformité européenne," French for "European conformity"). Here, the manufacturer attests that the appliance conforms to a set of rules. Failure to meet these standards means the appliance cannot be traded in the European Union (EU). It does not matter where the appliance was manufactured; if it lacks the CE seal, it is a no-go to be imported into the EU.

There is a key difference between UL-style seals and CE-style markings. The CE certification is granted when the product's *manufacturer* conforms to all the relevant performance and safety standards. However, the UL label is affixed by sending the product to a third-party tester, which verifies if the product conforms to the standards set by UL Solutions.

Standards and certifications like UL or CE work because they foster comprehensive testing. From dropping your toaster multiple times to hitting it with a ball to determining the degree of burned breakfast food with the help of a color chart broken down by waffle or toast, the standards are exhaustive, if not exacting.

This concept of a "seal" has been replicated in traditional cybersecurity. For instance, by doing a simple Google search, you can look up the different security standards that your favorite cloud provider adheres to. You can visit the manufacturer's page if you want to know the security checks your router has passed. Do you want to know how your bank's mobile app keeps your data safe? You can look that up, too. If an organization is adhering to a cybersecurity standard, it will most likely gloat about it.

But why gloat about it?

Standards simplify the selection process for consumers. Think of it this way: let's assume you know nothing about how a router works, and you have two choices: one router that has passed the safety and security checks and conforms to the International Standards Organization and another router without this seal of approval. Even if you know nothing about what went into the testing, you might be more likely to pick the one that has undergone some testing, even if you don't know what testing the routers have undergone.

Wouldn't it be comforting to see a sticker on your AI-controlled insulin pump certifying its algorithm is robust to adversarial manipulations? Wouldn't it be good to know that your bank conforms to a set of standards when using an algorithm to manage your retirement accounts? A sticker cannot prevent all accidents involving your toaster—one should still remove combustible crumbs, keep it away from the sink, and not dislodge one's toasted bagel with a fork. However, a sticker *does* certify that a standardized suite of rigorous tests has been performed that will dramatically reduce the chance of an electrical fire.

Standards for testing in AI should be no different. In fact, there is a wave of efforts attempting to build AI standards. In 2021 alone, 21 draft standards were released to tackle AI trust. By adhering to one or more of these standards, organizations can claim that they have cleared the AI safety or responsibility bar that the industry has agreed upon.

What's in it for the organization ultimately selling AI products?

First, there is perception. Organizations can seek out seals of approvals purely for competitive reasons. A seal of approval from these standards organizations could be seen as a seal of distinguishing factor. And anything that separates you from a competitor in a winner-takes-all AI dynamic would be sought after.

Next, there are favorable premiums from insurers. Insurance companies can nudge organizations to make prudent security choices. The most malignant attack an organization can face is receiving fake emails that lure recipients to part with passwords. It is the foundation on which all other attacks are built. Multifactor

authentication (MFA)—one-time codes or push notifications—
are powerful deterrents against these phishing attacks. MFA is so
good that just enabling it was responsible for blocking 100 percent
of probes from automated bots and 99 percent of bulk phishing
attacks on Google users' accounts. Today, many insurance provid-
ers will decline coverage for companies that have not enabled MFA.

Organizations already have cyber insurance to protect them from
traditional cyberattacks like ransomware and privacy breaches. The
answer was not straightforward when we explored whether existing cyber insurance policies would cover these newer adversarial
attacks on AI systems. Owing to the vacuum of security practices
in AI systems, insurance companies are wary of issuing policies at
reasonable premiums. This tracks to the early days of cyber insurance, when companies had lax security policies, thus allowing the
insurance market to be dominated by major insurance players with
sky-high premiums.

But one thing is clear from our research. Major insurers say that
any AI insurance they introduce will offer favorable premiums to
those who adhere to test and validate against one of the many AI
testing standards.

While at the outset, this might seem an arbitrary move by the
insurance companies, it makes business sense to favor organizations
complying with these AI testing standards. Insurance companies
epitomize data-driven decisions because actuarial tables and tomes
of historical data guide them. When they do not have a lot of data
for their actuaries—as is the case of attacks on AI systems—they
tend to buffer their risk to determine an appropriate premium to
remain profitable. So, organizations that willingly adopt these testing frameworks can at least show they have taken proactive steps
to secure their AI systems, thus earning favorable premiums from
insurance companies.

AI standards and certifications are an alluring market incentive. Their seal can be seen as a differentiator, can result in favorable premiums from insurers, and are a tried and tested formula
from cybersecurity testing. Because of this, they make for a simple
economic nudge. This addresses the second question in our quest,

"What appealing incentives may help organizations care more about AI security?"

But just because something is appealing does not mean it will be adopted.

Here Be the Most Crucial AI Law Ye've Nary Heard Tell Of!

How the United States and the EU approach AI systems certification reflects these regions' broader mindset. True to its laissez-faire approach to regulation, the United States is developing a voluntary AI risk management framework through the National Institute of Standards and Technology (NIST). Since NIST is nonregulatory, no one will be obligated to adopt this framework upon its release.

On the other hand, the EU is making the CE-style mark mandatory for what it considers high-risk AI systems, including those used in credit scoring or medical devices via the proposed Artificial Intelligence Act (AIA). The proposed AI Act even prompted the generally staid *MIT Technology Review* to dub it the "most important AI law you've never heard of." And there is a lot of truth to this hyperbole.

Remember in 2018, when you received a slew of emails with the subject "We have updated our privacy policy"? Even today, when you visit a random website, your first interaction may be to click the button to confirm that you "accept cookies." That's because the EU passed a privacy law called the General Data Protection Regulation (GDPR), stipulating how businesses should store and process EU citizens' personal data.

But perhaps you don't live in the European Union. Why did you receive those pesky emails, see those banners, and continue clicking that Accept Cookies button? Why should something passed in Brussels for the Europeans affect you, a non-European?

That's because of the *Brussels effect*. You see, the GDPR applies to any company that processes EU citizens' data, even those not operating in the EU. Consequently, by doing business in the EU or even just processing EU citizens' data, companies must adhere to the EU's GDPR, be they located in Brussels, Boston, or Brisbane. With the advent of the Internet, businesses are de facto global, so many opted to adhere to the new regulation. For an organization, it is more burdensome to build separate websites to comply with distinct EU and non-EU policies, so the changes are often rolled out to everyone worldwide. This was dubbed the Brussels effect by Columbia University professor Anu Bradford because the EU can make certain unilateral decisions for the rest of the world.

One reason you see those Accept Cookies buttons is that failure to adhere to the GDPR results in severe penalties. Organizations must pay up to $22 million or 4 percent of their *global* annual revenue—whichever is higher—underscoring that the EU has not limited its purview in scope or remuneration to Europe alone. Indeed, through February 2022, the EU has meted out 988 GDPR violations totaling $1.7 billion in fines. So, when it comes to the EU, regulations have teeth, and the EU is not afraid to bite.

The EU is now turning to AI with its Artificial Intelligence Act. This time, the fines are much higher than GDPR: rising to €30 million (about $31 million)—or 6 percent of global revenue—whichever is higher.

Still in draft stages in 2022, the AIA is the European Union's solution to curb harm from AI systems. The AIA pays particular attention to AI systems that could have devastating consequences for citizens, from wrongful arrests to financial ruin, particularly by groups underrepresented in AI datasets. The AIA would legislate additional guardrails for AI in high-risk scenarios and ban its use altogether in unacceptable applications. Certain high-risk applications will be required to get a CE-style verification mark.

The EU's AIA addresses the third puzzle piece in our quest. It is a forcing function for organizations to prioritize testing their AI systems for a wide array of properties. Because the act uses the testing framework as a nudge, it also taps into the market incentives for adoption. Incidentally, the AIA's properties are after the JASON group's "ilities"—reliability, maintainability, accountability, validity, debug-ability, evolvability, fragility, and attackability.

But—leading to the fourth question of our quest—why is it difficult and tricky to implement these properties? For this, we must analyze the trade-offs when securing AI and the challenges in implementing this sometimes vague regulatory compliance.

Lies, Accursed Lies, and Explanations!

"You don't want a Facebook internship?" Hima Lakkaraju's academic mentor double-checked with her in 2013. With her Stanford AI PhD, Lakkaraju was a shoo-in for any job her heart desired. But Lakkaraju had her fill of building commercial systems. She had already spent two years at IBM's AI division. Instead of another corporate stint, she chose academia and is today Professor Lakkaraju at Harvard, pushing the boundaries of helping humans understand AI's cryptic decisions.

AI systems are increasingly used in high-stakes domains. For example, in 2021 alone, the Food and Drug Administration authorized more than 30 AI-powered medical devices for clinical use. AI systems are now frequently used in pre-trial risk assessment— fancy speak for using AI to predict if someone should be granted bail. AI systems now control our finances, with banks already using machine learning models to predict if someone should be given a line of credit based on their financial history.

But how do we know these systems are working as intended? That's one of the "ilities" of the AI system: explainability. Essentially, when an AI system is explainable, the system attempts to provide how it reached a decision.

So, instead of yielding a simple "bail/no bail," "cancer/no cancer," or "loan approved/rejected" verdict, explainable AI systems provide a reason for reaching the decision. This way, humans overseeing the AI system's decisions could either render the final judgment or at least audit the system's decisions. For instance, a judge can look at the explanations from the AI system when determining whether someone should receive bail. Explainable AI also promises to aid regulators and policymakers. Should someone be denied a loan because of their race or gender, the AI explanation should clearly say so, and this would help policymakers take the appropriate legal remedy.

But there's just one problem: these explanations can be constructed to fool humans. To demonstrate this, Lakkaraju recruited 40 Harvard law graduates. These law-aware students knew that race and gender should not be included in any rationale for determining whether someone should receive bail. Lakkaraju showed participants the bail verdicts from three systems. The first option was a black-box system that simply provided a decision with no explanation. The second option was an AI system describing its decision along the lines of, "This person is risky for bail because their race is African American and their gender is male." The third was an AI system that explained, "This person is risky because they have committed a misdemeanor with a prior-arrests record and prior-jail-incarcerations." As one would expect, the to-be lawyers and to-be policymakers eschewed the black box, skipped the blatantly biased explanation, and instead preferred the third system whose explanation avoided prohibited features like race and gender.

But Lakkaraju had an ace up her sleeve. She constructed the third system to use *indirect* cues about race and gender, even though these did not appear explicitly in the explanation. Lakkaraju exploited the statistic that African American men are five times more likely to be jailed than their white counterparts. One out of every three Black males born today can expect to be sentenced to prison. Thus, African American men are more likely to have prior arrests and prior jail incarcerations. The "prior arrests" and "prior incarcerations" explanations resulted in outcomes similar to if the model had been allowed to use race and gender in the decision. Although the law students chose the explanation they thought did not use any protected attributes like race and gender, the model could "cheat" in its explanation by using highly correlated proxy attributes.

These sleight-of-hand attacks expose an incongruous reality: explainable AI systems touted as paragons of transparency, if not constructed correctly, would do little to engender trust. A policymaker, judge, or doctor cannot simply scan the explanation to ensure that AI systems are fair or equitable. Through intentional misleading or unintentional fumbling, producers of these explanations can construct them to trick humans.

This can be problematic. Despite overall faulty behavior from the AI system, if the explanation aligns with our worldview, we are likely to believe the explanation and rationalize the faulty behavior. They only further reinforce our biases without a critical eye evaluating the results. Lakkaraju deftly fooled the law experts by constructing explanations that specifically avoided gender and race, but in the background, the model was still tapping into them. "Bad explanations cause more harm than no explanations," Lakkaraju told us.

In a final plunge of the dagger, the very act of making AI systems explainable might also make them vulnerable to manipulation. One of the key challenges in poisoning attacks is knowing what to poison in a dataset for optimal results. Which data sample? The label or the image pixels? Indeed, knowing what to poison in a dataset is half the battle.

To disentangle this, Alina Oprea, the poisoning virtuoso we met in Chapter 4, turned to the very tool intended to describe machine learning's decision-making: explainability. She used explainability properties to identify factors a model considers important for a decision. For instance, to fool an antimalware system by poisoning, Oprea's research group first identified the most critical features of decision-making by employing explainability results. Using this insight, Oprea's lab was able to surgically craft malware that would create a blind spot in antimalware systems.

Exploiting ML explainability is the machine learning version of "gaming the system." If one knows that the loan algorithm is focused on the number of years in your current job, one might be tempted to fudge employment numbers just enough to get the loan approved. The tools that allow you to crack open the AI system for transparency can very much be used to crack the system itself.

No Free Grub

Broadly speaking, bias in an ML system occurs when it favors one outcome over another. This has already become an acute challenge as ML systems unfairly harm a subset of the population without a sense of equity and justice. The data used to train a system might underrepresent certain groups, and that social bias is then reflected in the model's performance. A landmark study led by Joy Buolamwini, Timit Gebru, and Deborah Raji showed that commercial facial recognition systems built by Amazon, Microsoft, and IBM consistently misrecognized people of color. The result? Over the years, wrongful arrests have been made in the United States using facial recognition evidence. All were wrongful arrests of Black men because the AI system misidentified them. Local governments began prohibiting the use of this technology, Amazon stopped selling these tools to law enforcement, and Microsoft recently stopped selling facial analysis tools altogether.

So, it is natural that the AIA is looking to mitigate societal bias in AI. But, again, things are not so straightforward as bias interacts with security unintuitively. Consider the adversarial attack example from Chapter 3, wherein carefully crafted distortion added to images causes a state-of-the-art AI system to misrecognize an image of a panda as a gibbon. See Figure 6-1.

"panda"   "gibbon"
57.7% confidence   99.3% confidence

Figure 6.1 When adversarial noise is added to an image of a panda, it is mistaken as a gibbon by ML systems. Courtesy of Ian Goodfellow14

When researchers from the University of Maryland repeated this attack method in facial recognition systems with a diverse set of faces, the impact of the attack on the faces was not uniform. The researchers showed that a small perturbation flipped the label for a Black female face, but a white male face was more robust to the same attack. Indeed, the same attack has varied results within a dataset across different image classes. It turns out that attacking Black female faces was easier than attacking white male faces. Researchers artificially constructed an ML system that predicts age from a face (the researchers explicitly acknowledge that this is an apocryphal task used merely for demonstration). The researchers then launched an adversarial example attack. At the end of the exercise, they found that they successfully changed the label (in this case age) of the Black female image but not the white male image. See Figure 6-2.

The rude irony in this situation is that, for the most part, these vulnerable data points from a security perspective also line up with vulnerable populations in the real world.

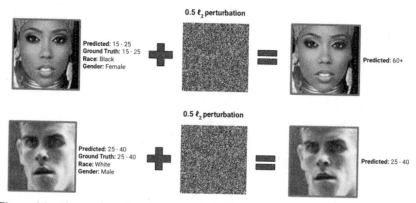

Figure 6.2   Researchers found that a Black female face is more susceptible to adversarial noise than a white male face. Courtesy of Vedant Nanda

There is a corresponding corollary to this finding: defenses do not protect all classes of data points equally. Researchers from Michigan State University showed that the same defense does not confer the same level of protection to all data points. One class in the dataset had a robust accuracy of 67 percent, while the other only had a robust accuracy of 17 percent.

So, does setting the same standard of defense for all data points, even within the same facial recognition task, make sense? Don't we want some of the more "vulnerable" data points to have additional layers of protection?

Insufficient technical solutions for explainability address one piece of our answer to the fourth question in our quest: why is it tricky to put these nudges in practice? The answer is that, there is no free lunch. There is mounting evidence showing that some of these properties conflict with each other. "Robust or Fair" is the title of one research paper detailing such a trade-off. You can have explainable AI systems or robust AI systems, but most likely, not both. You can have ML systems that are accurate at doing their tasks or robust to adversarial examples, but not necessarily both. So, you can have an AI system robust to stickers on the stop sign, but it might come at the cost of lowering the accuracy of identifying a pedestrian. If we rely only on AI systems, these are the trade-offs we might be forced to make.

But there are other reasons that the gap between standards and practice remains a chasm.

Whatcha measure be whatcha get!

In our experience of applying the draft EU framework for AI systems as a tabletop exercise—the most mature requirement so far—we hit several roadblocks. One of the checklist items from the proposed EU framework included this question: "Did you assess potential forms of attacks to which the AI system could be vulnerable?"

This question seems straightforward enough to a policymaker, but to an ML engineer, it is too vague to be useful. It would be like asking a homeowner to "verify that your residence is burglar-proof." Does a residence mean a townhome in Tennessee, a penthouse on Park Avenue, or a cabin in Colorado? Further, the guidance does not tell you *how* to burglar-proof the residence. Should one test the windows? Install cameras in the surroundings? Or install a moat with alligators? A world of choice leads to analysis paralysis.

In practice, no simple test applies to every AI system. Indeed, there is often not even a single ML model within an AI system! Instead, a network of interacting ML models works behind the scenes. A real-world search engine has tens to hundreds of ML models; your retirement account is likely governed by hundreds of ML models looking for everything from market volatility to understanding your risk preference. Should the entire system receive a single security assessment? Or should we score each ML model individually and then aggregate them?

Then there is the problem of when to do the assessment. When you buy a traditional oven, you know exactly what features it has, and these don't change. It does not magically one day gain the ability to pre-heat itself at 5:30 p.m. because it has learned that you make dinner every day at 6 p.m. But AI systems do routinely adopt similar behavior, which is part of their allure. They get smarter as you use them. So, for an engineer building these systems, should the assessment be done before releasing a new feature or every time the system learns about you? If tech companies are asked to do these assessments too often, it might block their ability to deliver value. If it's done too infrequently, then the security assessments could become stale and irrelevant.

Even if we were to get over these existential questions, checklists like those from the EU fail to hold any practical value. None of these AI risk-management frameworks gives practical guidance as to how a threat should be ameliorated. When interviewing teams about their needs for AI security, our conversations would often reach a dead end. "OK, I understand data poisoning. What software can I use to fix these problems?" The technical remedy is full of caveats and is generally unsatisfactory today. Even a company like Google acknowledges this, saying, "Currently, the best defenses against adversarial examples are not yet reliable enough for use in a production environment."

Standards present a dilemma. On the one hand, vague standards are practically difficult to implement. On the other hand, detailed standards that prescribe exactly what and how to test are also not a panacea. The dilemma is expertly stated by, management virtuoso, Thomas Johnson when addressing broad principles versus detailed controls. "Perhaps what you measure is what you get. More likely, what you measure is all you get. What you don't (or can't) measure is lost. By using quantitative targets to manage results . . . we close fields of possibility and limit ourselves to what our measures will produce."

Perhaps a good end state for principle-based standards is simply a mindset shift in the companies developing models. Today, still largely siloed ML engineering teams are separated from organizations that deal with governance, risk, and compliance. But, the shapeshifting and protean nature of adversarial machine learning defenses means security professionals need to be much more involved in the development phase. In a move to integrate security more into the development process, security professionals may help craft custom solutions for specific use cases and help organizations think of "risk tolerance" over binary "safe/unsafe" thinking.

So, who is going to make and resolve these trade-offs? Those building ML systems? The company's legal team? Standard organizations? Policymakers? A lot of this is left for interpretation, and there are no clear answers. That's the problem: the standards (our incentive) and the regulation (our forcing function) are both too vague to be practical.

Who Be Reapin' the Benefits?

"Cui bono?" That's what Cicero asked the court to consider when defending a wrongfully accused Roman citizen of patricide in 80 BC: "Who benefits?" he implored the court to reason how anyone can benefit from the enormous loss of their own father.

And so, we confront the final question in our quest, "Who benefits from testing and validating AI systems?"

Tech scholar Julie Cohen's book *Between Truth and Power* explains how the legal landscape is constantly stretched and pulled by corporations that stand to benefit from laws favorable to them. The same argument applies to standards. On the one hand, tech companies, which we surveyed to show that they are unaware of tools and processes to secure AI systems, were the loudest voices in the room when responding to and shaping AI standards. On the other hand, academia, which is exploding with adversarial AI research—publishing two papers every day since 2016—was muted.

After GDPR, U.S. companies spent $7.8 billion, most of which went to consulting firms and testing organizations. Sometimes, even accessing the standard—not to get certified—costs money. Want to download the standards noted on your toaster's compliance? Hope you have $500. Want a paper copy? Well, pony up about $1,000. And standards change all the time. You will have to pay for every revision. (Sometimes, you pay for the redline version, which highlights the proposed changes and shows the changed version.) Certainly, the entities that benefit most are consulting firms and standards-setting organizations themselves.

When it comes to the AIA, the cost is going to be bigger. Much bigger. The Center for Data Innovation, a nonpartisan technology think tank, estimated that the AIA "will cause an additional 17 percent of overhead on all AI spending" for organizations. This overhead is presumably to hire a fleet of consultants and lawyers and invest in a patchwork of technological tools to satisfy the regulation.

Corporations already fear these costs. If you want to know what keeps the CEO of a publicly traded company awake at night, look at Form 10-K, which the U.S. government requires every publicly traded company in the United States to submit. Not only does the form detail the company's financials, it is a compendium of the company's worst nightmares. In March 2022, NVIDIA, one of the biggest AI companies in the world, included remarkable words in its Form 10-K. Under the section "Risks Related to Regulatory, Legal, Our Stock, and Other Matters," NVIDIA, for the first time, mentioned regulation for the "responsible use of AI" as a factor that could increase the costs of adhering to the upcoming AI regulatory compliance.

While companies like NVIDIA might be able to bear this 17 percent overhead, small- and medium-sized businesses, which are the backbone of the AI economy, might not be able to brook this excess. Ultimately, this hurts the European economy. "By 2025, the AIA will have cost the European economy more than €30 billion," the report portends. While it is too early to say, companies may ultimately pass these costs down to consumers.

Beyond the monetary impact, AI systems bearing a seal will not nullify the possibility of AI failure. When was the last time you checked the seal of every electrical appliance you purchased? The stark reality is that most people who interact with AI systems won't know an AI system is behind the curtain, and even if they do, they might not have the means to discover what standards the AI system must comply with.

During a fire, are you going to stop and verify if the emergency robot has a CE marking? You simply have to trust that the very people in charge of building AI systems are adhering to the letter and spirit of these standards.

And that could be a problem in the winner-take-all dynamics of AI systems. Consider Telsa, which is the undisputed leader in the electronic vehicle category. It employs top-drawer ML engineers who lead the industry in self-driving vehicles. Objectively, Tesla has stellar safety ratings according to the U.S. government's own safety regulator. At one point, Tesla Model S did so well that it scored an impossible 5.4 on the 5-star rating, so the regulator had to revise the guidelines so cars couldn't surpass the 5-star rating.

Compare this with Tesla's qualitative signaling to its users. The *New York Times* reported that Tesla repeatedly "exaggerated the sophistication of Autopilot." Jennifer Homendy, chairwoman of the National Transportation Safety Board, told the *New York Times*, "Where I get concerned is the language that's used to describe the capabilities of the vehicle."

Research dating back to the 1990s repeatedly showed a pattern of overtrust in AI systems and automation. Organizations that build these systems have a heightened moral and ethical obligation to society to clearly communicate the limitations—especially when standards and regulations do not seem to hold technical or process merits.

Cargo Cult Science

So, where has our quest taken us? Where have our five questions guided our search for understanding? Economics suggest that companies are not incentivized to secure their AI systems. External incentives like the differentiation of a security-approved product and lower insurance premiums may be a gentle prod in the right direction. But, full-on regulatory compliance may still need time to mature in order to fully benefit the end user. Are we back where we started?

We argue no. The journey has made us wiser and stripped our eyes of the naïveté that blinded us. Let's unpack this further.

Allied Forces occupied remote islands during World War II to serve as strategic military bases. Island natives, who until then had little to no contact with the external world, now witnessed airplanes landing with supplies: everything from beefy tanks to clothing to medicines to canned food. This cargo also doubled as valuable trading commodities. When the army recruited the islanders to navigate the remote parts of the island, the army paid the islanders in cargo. The supplies enthralled the islanders, who soon came to associate the planes carrying the exotic cargo as a sign of cornucopia. But when the war ended, the countries packed their bags and moved away. Suddenly and abruptly, the planes stopped landing, and consequently, the cargo stopped flowing into the island.

The islanders were despondent over the disappearance of their precious cargo and wanted to woo the planes to get the supplies back. Their intent was indubitably pure. Using wood straw, sticks, and twine, they constructed their best imitations of the control towers and runways that once brought traffic to the island. In Vanuatu, islanders appealed each year to a mythical "John Frum" to bring back the planes. A chosen islander would wear American military regalia and walk around with a ceremonial gun, hoping the planes would land with cargo. One theory for the islanders' name: World War II servicemen may have introduced themselves as "John from. . . ."

From the islanders' point of view, these artifacts—wood towers and straw runways and wearing the uniform—would bring in the cargo they so coveted. Richard Feynman, the Nobel Prize–winning physicist, called this *cargo cult science* in his 1974 commencement speech at the California Institute of Technology.

Adversarial machine learning has its fair share of cargo cult science. Nicholas Carlini, who is proficient in breaking ML defenses, told us how scientists putting weak defenses fall prey to cargo cult: the defenses look like science, they pass some weak test, but in the end, they are as effective at making AI systems robust against attacks as straw runways are at bringing back planes.

Increasingly, regulators are building their own version of straw runways. They are confidently pushing for AI safeguards with the right appearance and intention but not the nuance or substance for implementation. For instance, the Federal Trade Commission argued for the penalty of "algorithmic disgorgement," such as removing algorithms trained on illegal data. That sounds reasonable at the outset: if a company trains on ill-gotten data, it must face the consequences. But the FTC's position on algorithmic disgorgement is quizzical. In the real world, an isolated ML model rarely acts alone. A scaffolding of engineering artifacts supports ML models. In lieu of a clear-cut separation, the ML models and the non-ML parts of the system meld into each other. Would the ML model and all its associated components that ingested bad data be removed? Or all ML models? Or will the entire system be disgorged? That's like bringing a machete to surgery.

"The premise is simple," the FTC commissioner and lawyers wrote in the *Yale Law Journal* when introducing algorithmic disgorgement. The FTC Commissioner's framing is akin to Elon Musk's remark that defending against adversarial examples is easy. Tech legal scholar Professor Tiffany C. Li examined the issue of algorithmic disgorgement and wrote in *SMU Law Review*: "Legal issues aside, the chief problem with algorithmic disgorgement is that it is not a particularly practicable solution." Li says the costs of disgorging entire AI systems are too dear and argues that this economic cost would "harm small startups and discourage new market entrants in technology industries." These are the very entities the FTC would like to foster and safeguard. The remedy, Li explains, doesn't lie in the hands of policymakers alone. "Ultimately, the debate around deletion should not center around data deletion, algorithmic deletion, or model deletion."

So, what is the solution here? Li proffers one: "What must be deleted is the siloed nature of scholarship and policymaking on matters of artificial intelligence."

Regulators, like the scientists building defenses, have good intentions: promote trust in AI. But like the islanders, many proposals, unfortunately, seem to be chasing artifacts that might not result in delivering desirable outcomes. For that, we must first accept that the "ilities" properties we seek—explainability, reliability, security, and more—are not isolated traits that can be enabled or disabled independently. Instead, they are deeply entangled and in tension with each other. We need to delete the siloed nature of the scholarship of seeking these properties individually; instead, we should achieve them holistically and practically.

The real question is not whether we need a framework with a testing regimen and sufficient enforcement mechanisms but how to develop one that inspires trust and promotes continued innovation.

That's a quest worth embarking on.

Chapter 7

The Big One

Chairman Thompson: "I am informed that you think that within 30 minutes, the 7 of you could make the Internet unusable for the entire nation. Is that correct?"

Those seven in question were Mudge, Weld Pond, KingPin, John Tan, Space Rogue, Brian Oblivion, and Stefan Von Neuman.

You would be correct in thinking that those seem like made-up names. The seven were from a Boston–based hacker group called L0pht (pronounced "loft") Heavy Industries. Their operations were conducted in a makeshift loft (hence the name) filled with gadgets, gizmos, and the quaint—a sort of geeky thrift store complete with mannequins wearing gas masks. It was their haven for breaking into everything from manual locks to computer desktops. The *Washington Post* described their lair aptly as a "computer fraternity-cum-high tech clubhouse."

Renting a Dodge Ram 3500 15-passenger van and donning their borrowed or newly purchased suits, the hacker group took a road trip from Boston to the nation's capital to brief the U.S. Senate. The group used aliases instead of their real names because they all had regular day jobs and did not want their employers to know about their side hustle of hacking into computers. As hackers who operated near the law's boundary, they were skeptical of the government and, hence, did not want to broadcast their real names. L0pht even booked their hotel rooms in Washington, DC, using their aliases, much to the chagrin of the front desk.

But no one really cared about their names. It was their security knowledge that was of interest. In a blockbuster hearing entitled "Weak Computer Security in Government: Is the Public at Risk?" the group assembled in front of the senators to patiently answer their questions on the topic. Between Mudge's flowy feral mane and Brian Oblivion's blonde shoulder locks, it was the most peculiar sight among the staid DC crowd—almost a Hollywood stereotype of socially awkward geeks. The entire affair would have appeared staged if not for the chairman of the Senate Committee on Governmental Affairs, Senator Fred Thompson from Tennessee, donning an unremarkable gray suit and unremarkable hairdo, gaveling in the session.

That was in May 1998. Decades later, some things have changed: being a geek is now rather cool, and computer security is now kitchen table conversation. But some things have also remained the same.

The L0pht group's testimony applies to artificial intelligence as much as to any emergent technology. "If you are looking for computer security, the Internet is not the place to be," the L0pht group warned the U.S. government. "The technology is being asked to perform tasks it was never intended to."

Despite AI's pitiable security, we are asking it to perform high-stakes tasks today that should require rigor never conceived or intended by this technology.

So, where do we go from here? What is the future of ML systems, especially when defenses are still nascent, inconclusive, or incomplete and when policy guidance is abstract at best?

Experts like us authors, who deal with securing AI systems daily, might make for the worst prognosticators of what will happen in the future. Blinded by our own myopia, we are more likely to miss other signals. So, taking take a page from *Superforcasting*, a book authored by Wharton professor Philip Tetlock and journalist Dan Gardner, we spoke to hundreds of stakeholders in security and AI. This ranged from upper management to front-line professionals, from medical doctors to U.S. career diplomats to data scientists, from researchers to agriculturists employing AI, from policy wonks to venture capitalists. Then, to look at what's on the horizon, we analyzed the path of our Internet elders and translated their battle scars from combating malicious bits and bytes for years to lessons that we parvenus can learn about the ways of AI safety.

After all, while history might not repeat itself, it most definitely rhymes.

This Looks Futuristic

Chairman Thompson (1998): "You say that you have been working with some governmental agencies with regard to some of these problems and, of course, with commercial entities. What occurs to me in listening to you and listening to our prior witness is that there does not seem to be an inducement for industry to do much about this at this stage of the game. That is what you are saying, essentially, is it not?"

Mr. MUDGE. "Yes."

In 2018, at the height of adversarial machine learning interest in academia, we wanted to know how organizations were thinking about securing their AI systems. After all, by this time, even the flagship organizations heavily investing in AI systems—Microsoft, Google, Amazon, Facebook, IBM, and Tesla—had encountered some form of failure in their AI systems. We saw contemporary movement in the standards and regulations space addressing safety and security. We thought the combination of rife failures and forthcoming regulation should be sufficient to induce organizations to proactively prepare to defend against system attacks. It aligned with Anderson's economic motivations for Internet security, which might reasonably transfer to AI security as well.

But we were wrong. Terribly wrong.

Based on interviews with more than 80 organizations across the globe, spanning two years, we found that more than 95 percent of organizations were woefully unprepared to defend their AI systems from attacks. These included large companies—names you would

NOT WITH A BUG, BUT WITH A STICKER

recognize, major banking institutions, producers of AI-powered home appliances that you are likely to own, manufacturers of popular smart devices, and makers of common cars.

The jarring inference was that most organizations did not have a process in place to systematically test their AI systems for failures. Think about that. From the AI system powering your smart vacuum cleaner to the AI system serving you ads to the one diagnosing your health to driving you around, it is unlikely to have been systematically tested for robustness against adversarial manipulation.

Except for a sparing few, most organizations lack a playbook to execute when their AI system fails from a poisoning attack, when its performance is degraded, or if the ML system is stolen. Should an attack unfold today on AI systems, the bulk of industry would not just be left scrambling; they would not even know it happened.

More than the lack of knowledge, the self-deception was troubling. Regarding attacks on AI systems, one of the cybersecurity analysts we spoke to from a large bank remarked, "This looks quite futuristic."

At the 2022 RSA—arguably the security industry's largest conference—after a presentation on attacking ML systems from academic researchers, an attendee walked to the mic and asked, "Why should I care? Most of this is [just] research anyway."

But that's not how others see it.

The UK government, somewhat echoing themes in the NSCAI report, proclaimed, "All aspects of an AI or ML system's security are potentially vulnerable, and compromises of system confidentiality, integrity, and availability have all been previously observed." For governments, the compromise of AI systems is not a hypothetical "if" but a response from practical experience.

Or consider the 2022 Senate hearing on artificial intelligence from the Armed Services Subcommittee. Eric Horvitz, the Chief Scientific Officer at Microsoft, got a curve ball that would have flummoxed most: the senators asked Horvitz to explain the difference between a computer program, machine learning, artificial intelligence, and quantum computing to the committee, adding that Horvitz would need to dumb the answers down to the senator's kindergarten understanding of technology. Oh, Horvitz also had one minute for this question. Horvitz has 30 years of AI research under his belt and is one of the most feted ML researchers, so he knocked the ball out of the park. Andrew Lohn—who posited that adversarial examples might be a valuable arrow in the AI security quiver (see Chapter 1)—was sandwiched between Horvitz and Andrew Moore, Director of Google Cloud AI. Lohn has the distinction of discussing adversarial examples in the U.S. Senate in a public hearing for the first time.

Moore's banter with a senator during a routine Q&A stood out. "This notion that folks can actually poison our own systems was kind of 'science fiction' five years ago, but it has happened to me, and I have been on the front lines of dealing with this and attacks against Google systems. So, as you can imagine, that is now a major aspect of defense." To the armed services subcommittee, Moore lifted adversarial machine learning from the realm of science fiction to reality.

There is another plausible reason NSCAI was tuned to the threats to AI systems: Moore and Horvitz testified at the hearing and served as NSCAI commissioners.

The concept of AI red teams—dedicated teams proactively finding failures in AI systems, like the one used in Area 52 (see Chapter 1)—is now emerging in the industry. Google, Facebook, Microsoft, and NVIDIA—top AI companies—all have one.

But don't measure the industry by what the big AI kahunas are doing. The NSCAI correctly noted, "With rare exceptions, the idea of protecting AI systems has been an afterthought in engineering and fielding AI systems, with inadequate investment in research and development."

Why is that? Why is there a disconnect in the rest of the industry?

By All Means, Move at a Glacial Pace; You Know How That Thrills Me

Just because an attack is possible doesn't mean it will happen. After all, AI systems are more likely to fail due to common errors than because of a malicious adversary actively trying to subvert them. When it comes to safety and security, Murphy (shorthand for Murphy's law) more commonly rears his head than Mallory (the canonical malicious person in security textbooks). Nevertheless, as the dominant and prevailing technology of our time, why aren't organizations racing to be in front of this problem? We suggest three probable causes for this languor.

- First, organizations tend to have a romanticized view of attackers as hackers in hoodies working in front of glowing computers with scrolling green text. They prioritize nation-state actors over the more commonplace script-kiddy attacker, even though the latter might have a higher likelihood of infiltrating their systems. As discussed in this book, in reality, adversaries come in varying stripes, and even unsophisticated attacks can be potent to the average person. The Chinese government evading Twitter's antispam algorithm with simple random characters, is on the same level of sophistication as Tumblr users coloring adult images green to evade porn filters. Organizations should broaden their definition of failure and loosen (if not lose) their obsession with a particular type of adversary.
- Next, awareness about the brittle security guarantees of AI systems is at an all-time low. In their 1988 testimony, the hacker group highlighted that the abysmal state of Internet security was compounded by the lack of education in this area and a complete lack of awareness of this topic. According to a survey by the Allen Institute for AI, 84 percent of Americans are essentially AI illiterate. Most Americans lack a nuanced understanding of how AI systems work, fostering blind trust in black-box models. Congress found this so jarring that it allocated significant funding in the 2021 National Defense Authorization Act to at least educate senior Department of Defense executives about AI and emerging technologies.
- Lastly, organizations are just not, well, organized to think about these problems. In his book *Industry Unbound*, Professor of Law and Computer Science at Northeastern University Ari Ezra

Waldman showed how tech companies were so stovepiped and Kafkaesque that it unintentionally weakened data privacy. This way, even a well-meaning developer who wants to take privacy seriously must wade through complex corporate hierarchy and work through office politics. These privacy champs are set up to give up.

Indeed, part of the failure to secure AI is organizational structure, in a manifestation of what's come to be known as Conway's law: "Any organization that designs a system will produce a design whose structure is a copy of the organization's communication structure." Indeed, security and AI teams were distinct in all organizations we spoke to. Teams reported to the security leader, nominally called the chief information security officer (CISO), and teams reported to the chief data officer, the leader of AI initiatives. Our interviews found that these two suborganizations rarely communicated about AI security. This presents a dilemma: data office staffers, who might be better informed about attacks on AI systems, do not have the security mandate, so they cannot purchase security-related solutions or unilaterally issue security directives in their organizations. Meanwhile, security professionals, who have the authority, either are unaware of the problem or are more focused on other priorities.

To some extent, the U.S. government, which cares most about securing AI systems than any other organization that we have spoken to, has led the way in establishing organizational clarity. The newly created Chief Digital and Artificial Intelligence Office (CDAO) brings together a variety of specialists—from experts in machine learning to experts in securing these systems under the same roof. The entire office is made a priority at the Pentagon, with direct reporting to the deputy secretary of defense.

Indeed, when it comes to adversarial machine learning, the industry can learn a lot from the U.S. government.

With the sobering results of our survey, we wanted to know what would help organizations spring into action. When will they begin to care about vulnerable AI systems?

Waiting for the Big One

Chairman Thompson (1998): "While advances in computing power are creating many opportunities in business and are remaking how the government does business and such things as how future wars are fought, it also creates dangers which must be reduced. It seems that the more technologically advanced we become, the more vulnerable we become."

Replace the words *computing power* in that statement with *AI* in these 1998 remarks, and you have the gist of this book. Even without alteration, one could even argue that the statement from Senator Thompson applies to us in the age of AI. Andrej Karpathy, then director of AI at Tesla, famously quipped that AI is software 2.0—a pithy way of saying AI systems are just an evolution of traditional computers and coding. And since it is an evolution, there is an element of inheritance. Most notably, AI inherits the vulnerabilities of the traditional computing paradigm. So, the lessons taught to the U.S. Senate in 1998 still ring true.

That's good news. And that's bad news. It's good news because we know what to expect. But it's bad news because few are doing something about it. In our interviews, we asked organizations what it would take for them to care about securing AI systems. One CISO frankly told us, "After the big one hits."

In the Pacific Northwest, the geological "big one" might be the impending earthquake that is supposed to swallow the entire region; in the Rockies, it might be the super volcano that is overdue for an eruption. What is the "big one" for AI security?

To put it bluntly, everything will change when a high-profile attack on an AI system makes it to the front page of the *New York Times*. The "big one" would set in motion the transformation of adversarial machine learning from a largely academic topic to a headlining buzzword. First, it will make a stir in idea festivals hosted by the likes of the World Economic Forum and the Aspen Institute. It will then trickle down to tech influencers at SXSW, where it will get a "zippy" name that vendor booths in trade shows will co-opt. Ultimately, it will percolate into buying guides from market research reports, which will package what is accessible largely only to academic researchers into information and tooling accessible to practitioners via premium offerings that cost tens of thousands of dollars. Indeed, only after the market research guides market the "the big one" will most companies begin to invest in actively securing AI systems, partially for consumer and self-protection and partially for fear of missing out.

If you think that it would be too late to think about security after a lot of people start using the system, you are right. But unfortunately, security has often been home to a "cross that bridge when we come to it" mentality. The reality is that chief security officers responsible for securing the systems in an organization have a limited budget and already have a long list of things to do. AI is not on their radar; therefore, today, it is not part of their bailiwick. It's not because they don't care about securing AI systems; instead, they are busy caring more about other things.

The "big one" as an external stimulus is somewhat a free-market perspective on how companies will self-correct to adopt AI security. In Chapter 6, we also learned that because organizations are incentivized by prevailing economics to deliver insecure products, the market may require intervention through standards, seals of approval, and even regulatory compliance, provided that it is drafted thoughtfully, slowly, and without the naïveté of a cargo cult. These conditions are not mutually exclusive. The "big one" is likely to happen regardless of whether there is intervention through public policies to achieve AI security. But diligent efforts to self-regulate may limit the blast radius.

So, what are some candidates for the big one? When contemplating candidates, it's useful to consider both the attack's impact and the attacker's profile. We will take a brief detour to the traditional cybersecurity attacks timeline.

The impact of the big one might be on the scale of a major cybersecurity breach. In the late 1990s and early 2000s, newsworthy cybersecurity attacks had already happened. For example, 15-year-old Jonathan James famously breached the U.S. Department of Defense. Another 15-year-old with the appellation MafiaBoy caused a widespread denial-of-service attack on a number of high-profile commercial systems, including Amazon, CNN, eBay, and Yahoo! However, the first large-scale (as measured by the number of people impacted) cybersecurity data breaches occurred in March 2005. This was the first known data breach to compromise more than 1 million records, including credit card numbers and names, at big-box footwear retailer Designer Shoe Warehouse. This initial explosion echoed louder with a subsequent breach only a few months later. In June, attackers stole 40 million credit card accounts from payment card processor CardSystems Solutions. Despite the impact of the breaches, many companies were slow to improve their own cybersecurity practices—after all, they weren't storing any credit card data, so they probably weren't attractive targets for fraudsters.

Then came a turning point in the awareness of cybersecurity breaches because of public awareness about the threat actors behind the breaches. In April 2014, cybersecurity firm Mandiant released a report boldly exposing the Chinese People's Liberation Army cyber espionage group, known as Unit 61398, for their intrusions in nearly 150 victims over 7 years. In August, the largest breach of all time occurred when attackers compromised all 3 billion Yahoo! user accounts that didn't include credit card information; instead, the data included names, email addresses, telephone numbers, dates of birth, and some security question and answer data. These data were attractive to a different sort of adversary. Investigators believe Russia's Federal Security Service (FSB) was responsible for the breach, which used stolen data to spy on a range of targets in the United States, including White House and military officials.

Given all this cybersecurity context, the big one is unlikely to come from an attacker using a sticker on a stop sign to cause your Tesla to confuse the stop sign for a yield sign. It is unlikely to be from your Amazon Alexa getting tricked by an audio adversarial example. Instead, the big one will come from the subversion of a high-stakes AI model. It might include stolen data or gravely wrong predictions, but it will affect millions in either case.

But today, we are still in the early days of ML attacks. On the traditional cyberattack timeline, we are still pre-1999 regarding the observed impact of attacks against AI. The threat is real—but the big one is yet to come. And in our low-security state of AI today, one early candidate for the big one might also be launched through "traditional" security attack vectors.

Software, All the Way Down

Several dozen taxis flooded Russia's Fili district, a busy west-central neighborhood in Moscow. Attackers had compromised Yandex Taxi, Russia's largest cab service, and sent a message requesting all available taxis to come to the same address in the heart of the city. The result: chaos and traffic jam. No fancy stickers. No advanced adversarial machine learning. Just traditional hacking.

Then there is the case of insider threats wherein employees steal AI trade secrets which Tesla and Apple's secret autonomous car division fell prey to. In both cases, it was when the company's engineers left for a Chinese autonomous vehicle startup—XPeng, their direct competitor. Despite Apple's infamous policies to keep its plans secret, an engineer simply "AirDropped" 24 gigabytes of Apple's autonomous car plans onto his wife's laptop. In Tesla's case, an engineer uploaded the source code relating to the Autopilot technology to his iCloud account before leaving for the Chinese company. Once again, there was no fancy machine learning attack to re-create the algorithm. It was simple stealing.

Even coordinated attacker groups are getting into the fray. NVIDIA and AMD, AI hardware manufacturers, both were victims of ransomware attacks. In the case of NVIDIA, a treasure trove of information was released by attackers: from detailed product plans to schematics to circuit diagrams. Semiconductor analyst Dylan Patel called it "a national security disaster." The public release of these documents, he posited, "With this data, the multiple Chinese AI and GPU [general processing units] firms can kickstart and catch up massively on the design of their GPUs." Again, it was run-of-the-mill traditional cyber attacks, not fancy ML attacks.

These three instances are a good reminder that machine learning is built with software. AI might seem like math and magic, but under the hood, AI runs on bits and bytes. And software will inevitably be exploited. Traditional software hacking methods get the job done without resorting to adversarial machine learning.

This line of thought—exploiting software—is particularly germane given AI's reliance on open-source communities. In 1984, Turing Award winner Ken Thompson asked a provocative question: to what extent can we trust computer programs? In his 15-minute lecture at the award ceremony—this is not the Oscars, where the band starts playing after 30 seconds—Thompson's answer was unequivocal: "The moral is obvious. You can't trust code that you did not totally create yourself." The point was that if you are using a product that is running code that someone else had written, you should assume it should be compromised.

A viable antidote for this is open-source software. You might think machine learning engineers are writing custom AI software for each application, building everything from first principles. But in reality, they are assembling systems, like a chef combining ingredients instead of making their own salt, growing their own peppercorns, and milling their own flour.

All this comes at a cost. As XKCD cartoon creator Randall Munroe put it in his illustration titled "Dependency," modern digital infrastructure rests on a precarious Jenga tower supported by a single project "some random person in Nebraska has been maintaining thanklessly since 2003." In other words, most modern software, including AI systems, depends on other pieces of software that sometimes a single person maintains. This might seem incredulous, but fewer than 10 developers wrote 90 percent of the code for some of the most widely used open-source packages in 2021. So, when one person chooses to act erratically, everything breaks down.

Indeed, that point of failure manifested in early January 2022. Marak Squires, the developer of a popular program for displaying colorful fonts, became irate that large corporations used his libraries without paying for his work. So, he decided to corrupt them on purpose. He changed his library to display "Liberty, Liberty,

Liberty," a cartoon of Uncle Sam, and the American flag and then go into an endless loop, causing some systems to use the code to become unresponsive. Because Squires' software offered a fundamental functionality—displaying fonts in different colors—many people became dependent upon it and built other software. His program had 20 million weekly downloads. So, when Squires decided to corrupt his program, he corrupted millions of software projects, including those of Amazon and Facebook. Many suddenly crashed and became unresponsive.

The other problem is that many dependencies might be old (this is the "2003" in Munroe's joke) and are not up-to-date with plugging their security holes. When the Log4j library was found to have a serious security hole, Jen Easterly, the director of the U.S. Department of Homeland Security (DHS) Cybersecurity and Infrastructure Security Agency (CISA), called it "the most serious vulnerability I've seen in my decades-long career." Easterly's comments were no hyperbole. Within 12 hours of the vulnerability being known, 20,000 attacks were launched. Within 72 hours, the number swelled to 800,000 attack attempts. Checkpoint research, which compiled these numbers, called it a *cyber pandemic*. More than 90 countries and 50 percent of corporate networks were affected by this vulnerability. It truly was most serious. Attackers of all stripes—from high school champs all the way to sophisticated attackers—were attempting to exploit this vulnerability in the open-source software library.

Its reliance on an open-source ecosystem makes AI systems especially susceptible to supply chain attacks. We have already seen how adversaries can poison data and ML models—these are novel to ML systems. But bugs in open-source AI software are existing vulnerabilities inherited from the traditional space. This does not mean AI systems should move away from open-source software. That would be disruptive and untenable. Instead, we can start with better incentives for those maintaining open-source software to take security seriously.

The Aftermath

Chris Darby, president and CEO of In-Q-Tel, relayed to us how he thinks about the big one for AI systems. Darby is responsible for investing in startups that further the U.S. intelligence services' mission. Darby has a reputation for having an uncanny ability to read the future. Darby was also an NSCAI commissioner. During his stint as NSCAI commissioner, he advocated for microelectronics and biotechnology as areas the commission should explore for America to sustain its AI leadership. Others in the commission, including Bajraktari, were skeptical if it really was the mandate of the NSCAI to wade into these "out there" areas. Lo, and behold, in 2020, when the pandemic hit, two of Darby's predictions came true. First, we faced a microelectronics shortage that greatly stupefied AI's ability. Simultaneously, researchers turned to AI as a tool to respond to the COVID-19 crisis.

Darby's take on AI's big one is uniquely American—and right on the money. He believes the big one will be when a class action lawsuit erupts from an AI system failure. Darby's prediction of AI systems has already manifested in traditional security. When the American Medical Collection Agency (AMCA), a debt collector for medical labs, suffered a data breach in 2019, it immediately faced a series of lawsuits—ultimately declaring bankruptcy. Soon after, 41 U.S. states sued AMCA and were awarded $21 million. As part of the settlement, AMCA was allowed to operate as long it took security seriously and opened itself to security assessments.

Darby's prediction could first manifest in the EU, where the EU's Artificial Intelligence Act (AIA) has a corresponding liability component. This means consumers can sue the AI system manufacturer if certain kinds of AI systems fail—either through intentional interference by an adversary or an unintentional failure. This will set up a legal showdown worthy of all the popcorn.

Chris Wysopal, who went by Weld Pond at the U.S. Senate hacker hearing in 1998 and is now the cofounder of the security company Veracode, reasoned about the big one a little differently. Wysopal up-leveled the discussion even further. "The big one is that which harms trust," he told us. It is possible, Wysopal thinks, the big one might be a series of breaches that could chip away at our trust in AI systems.

Thanks to a series of breaches in the traditional security space, nobody is under the impression that the Internet is secure today. The Centre for International Governance Innovation surveyed more than 20,000 people around the globe on how they perceive Internet security and trust in 2017. Twenty-two percent of the respondents said they avoided shopping online because they did not have enough trust in security measures. Even the military avoids the Internet for highly critical applications.

Ultimately, what the big one turns out to be—compromise via open-source software, a series of breaches, or a class action lawsuit—might not matter. The final result would be seismic none-theless: consumers will lose trust in AI systems after the big one, which could take years to rebuild.

Race to AI Safety

Chairman Thompson (1998): "I am curious. If a foreign government was able to assemble a group of [people] such as yourselves and paid them large amounts of money and got them in here or hired them to wreak as much havoc on this government, how much damage could they do?"

Mr. Space Rogue: "We would be in trouble."

Each year, we participate in an invitation-only workshop hosted by the UK government on securing AI systems, where we have a grounded discussion on adversarial machine learning with a group of brilliant researchers mixed with wry British sarcasm. Each year, participation has steadily increased. First, it was Canada who joined in on the workshop. Next came the U.S. government with its panoply of three-letter agencies.

There is a stark difference between how we talk about this topic to commercial organizations versus how we speak with govern-ments. For business executives, we begin by convincing them why securing AI systems is important. We then demonstrate how their

AI systems—the perceived crown jewels of their organizations, the ones in which their organization pays NFL-style salaries to build— are fallible, especially at an adversary's hands.

But governments we have spoken to catch on instantly. There is no need to persuade them that this is an emergent problem they should care about. Governments worldwide have a graduate-level appetite for this topic, while most companies still eat at the kids' table. One rationale is that sophisticated AI systems from the government will invite sophisticated attackers. Governments need to prepare for that eventuality.

The trouble for the U.S. government's AI systems will most likely stem from China. When it comes to research about attacking and securing AI systems, China is neck and neck with the United States. In our interviews, multiple experts repeatedly stressed that framing AI as an arms race, where there is a single definite winner, is not productive.

One thing, however, is certain: the country that secures its AI systems will have two obvious advantages. First, the country can ensure that its critical AI systems—from defense to healthcare— are appropriately protected from adversarial manipulation. Also, as a byproduct, the country would reap the benefit of protection from unintentional failures. This will lead to a wider trust among its citizens that the AI systems work as intended, leading to better adoption. Second, the country will also have a leg up in attacking ML systems since hardening from these attacks also naturally provides insights into how these systems can be exploited.

But a third advantage will also be conferred upon a nation that can secure its own AI systems: a leg up in diplomacy. Helen Toner, Director of Strategy at Georgetown's Center for Security and Emerging Technology, is an expert in China-U.S. AI affairs, especially regarding AI safety. In 2021, Toner and her colleague noted, "Preventing AI accidents could even be an opportunity for engagement with China, which faces the same accident risks as other AI powers."

There is a precedent for this kind of sharing: Permissive Action Links (PAL). At the height of the Cold War, tensions between the United States and the Soviet Union were running high. And there was the possibility of firing nuclear weapons without the president's knowledge: either from an irate insider to the threat of one of the allies taking issues into their own hands and deploying the nuclear weapons that the United States has placed in their care. So, in 1962, President John F. Kennedy signed a memorandum to ensure that all these nuclear weapons were to be secured using PAL, a cryptographic lock. Essentially, if an unauthorized user entered an incorrect code too many times, the nuclear weapons would not work. Not only did the U.S. deploy PAL widely in its own nuclear arsenal, but it was also said the United States should distribute this technology to Russia since it was in United States' interest to keep all nuclear weapons safe.

There are some kinks when using the PAL analogy in the context of AI security. For one, just because a technology is available doesn't mean countries will adopt it. Until the 1990s, despite PAL being available for 30 years, the UK's nuclear arsenal in submarines was protected using bicycle locks. Some countries refused the technology because they thought the United States backdoored it. This brings into focus whether AI safety would ultimately be seen as a viable bargaining chip.

For now, China appears uninterested in engaging with the United States on AI safety. The U.S. State Department has reached out to China multiple times on this front, but calls for cooperation have gone unanswered. The U.S.-Russia talks on AI were making a modicum more progress until that also hit a dead end when Russia invaded Ukraine. Instead, Toner's observation might manifest first with U.S. allies. Most prominently, the Quad—shorthand for India, the United States, Japan, and Australia—has already pledged integrated technical relationships. Maybe that could evolve into including AI safety as well.

One thing is certain. The country that makes headway in securing AI systems will have a trio of decisive advantages: protecting its own AI assets, exploiting an adversarial nation-state's AI assets, and deploying AI safety as a diplomatic tool.

Happy Story

Senator Glenn (1998): "Could you get in and transfer federal reserve funds to someplace?" Mr. Mudge. "Just about everything is possible."

It was a decommissioned airport runway, and the action was palpable. A 2009 Chevy Impala was trying to reach the end of the flight strip, but it couldn't, not for lack of trying but because another car was driving in parallel and actively trying to sabotage it. But unlike *The Fast and Furious* movie franchise, there was no physical interference. No headbutting. No T-boning. The interference was all digital.

Yoshi Kohno, then a graduate student at the University of Washington, along with Stefan Savage from the University of California San Diego in 2010, led the first-ever exploration of what it means to hack a car from a distance.

Convincing the world that this was a threat was an uphill battle. When the work was eventually presented at the famous Oakland Security conference—the one that got Ross Anderson to think about the economics of security—Kohno and the group faced a tough crowd. Just as Papernot would face in the future when trying to publish work on adversarial machine learning, the audience was highly skeptical. The critics did not seem to consider Kohno's team's work relevant. The critics said cars and computer security are like oil and water; they just don't mix. Worse still, they did not consider it "pure" security work like one would consider cryptography. Why spend time on an attack vector that was not there yet? Their peers pointed out that no one is going to hack cars by tapping into their networks. This might be a threat, but it is not sufficiently dire to be worth exploring, the critics piled on. The overwhelming sentiment was clear: let's focus on the immediate security needs and prioritize securing the Internet and traditional desktop computers.

But the stars aligned, and the word that a ragtag group of academic researchers hacked Impalas reached the car's manufacturer, General Motors. These researchers were invited for a show-and-tell.

When this academic team showed up at General Motors, they did what all academicians do when they give presentations: go through the gory detail of their methodology. Think a wall of text on white-background slides. But then, toward the end of their presentation, the researchers turned on the windshield wipers, blared the horns, played music, and caused the parked car on the curb to move—all from the confines of the conference room. General Motors was stunned. This was a real threat. In record time, General Motors appointed a vice president of security to take car hacking seriously. In what would later be seen as an inflection point, other car companies followed suit.

DARPA, the vanguard in bringing moonshot projects to fruition, kicked off an effort to ensure that cyber-physical systems can be trustworthy. NTHSA, the organization responsible for vehicular safety and currently investigating failures in Tesla, added first-ever security guidelines for car manufacturers, despite being among the skeptics who questioned Kohno's work.

This is a happy story for everyone. Academic researchers unveiled never-before-seen threats. Car companies responded with collective, concrete, and clear action and the U.S. government responded with investments and regulation, that all together staunched this security threat. Skepticism about the viability of these security threats was real, but no one waited around for the first big attack on cars to appear on the front page of the *New York Times*. No one waited for the threat of class-action lawsuits or the threat of inducements. No one waited around for lives to be lost because a car's security was compromised. No one was a dogmatic denier.

Ten years later, the Oakland conference that was once tepid to this work gilded Kohno and the entire team with their most prestigious award: the "Test of Time" honor. Kohno would go on to become a computer science professor at the University of Washington and eventually advise a student, Ivan Evtimov, on formulating the famous "stop sign" attack against self-driving cars.

The moral is obvious: if we pay attention to the early warnings from academic researchers, we can prevent threats before they cause widespread damage. We can avert disasters.

In Medias Res

Senator Lieberman (1998): "Senator Thompson indicated that somebody had referred to you as rock stars of the new computer age. It is probably not what you came to hear, but actually, I think you are performing an act of very good citizenship, and I appreciate it. I hope you do not mind that I am not going to call you rock stars. I would compare you more to Rachel Carson, who sounded some early warnings about what environmental pollution was doing to the environment, and in the defense context, you might be modern-day Paul Revere, except, in this case, it is not the British coming. We do not know who is coming."

Mr. MUDGE: "Right. You have got it."

"Rage—sing, goddess, of the rage of Peleus' son, Achilles, that ruined all the Acheans."

So begins Homer's *The Iliad*. We are never told why Achilles is angry or why his wrath is calamitous. Nor how Achilles' fury proved ruinous to all. We are just dropped in the middle of the action, left to find our footing as the epic poem rushes and races through the battleground.

But as we work through the 15,693 lines of dactylic hexameter, we are rewarded with the complete picture. We are given Achilles' entire backstory and the events that led to the ruinous rage and the events thereafter. What started as chaotic abandonment by Homer when he dropped us in the middle of his poem unspools, beautifully conveying the past, present, and future.

The literary technique of starting in the middle is called "in medias res," which translates literally to "the midst of." And once you learn to spot in medias res, you see it everywhere, from Milton to Marvel movies, from Dante to daytime TV dramas.

In medias res works as a tool for another important reason. Not only is the backstory fascinating, but also because the future story is worth telling. Indeed, we believe AI's future is filled with hope and optimism. We have pointed out that securing AI systems is not a novel conversation. So long as there are computers, there will be vulnerabilities. The sooner we know about them, the more time we have to prepare.

Fortunately, the minds and eyes of hundreds of AI researchers are shining a light on their limitations before an adversary can point them out to us. These AI researchers are our modern-day Paul Reveres and Rachel Carsons, pointing out the imminent challenges before we become dependent on flawed technology in too many high-stakes applications. Their acts of good citizenship provide us valuable time and foreknowledge to correct course, to innovate technically, and to grapple with standards, norms, and policies that, together, will help us trust these systems with "justified confidence."

To that end, rather than prognosticating potential outcomes, we conclude with a call to action. Because the best outcomes will require contributions from technologists, business leaders, civil rights activists, policy wonks, and the persuasion of educated consumers, let us work together to secure AI systems with mindful dispatch. We should all have ample motivation as AI adoption spreads into so many facets of our lives. And so, we must take concomitant action.

We are in medias res with learning how attacks on AI systems happen. It is all but certain that because of ML systems' pervasiveness and criticality, attacks on them will spread. What was once considered an outlier will become commonplace. But for now, we are gifted a period of calm to prepare before these embers in the smithy swell to a malevolent global conflagration that could torch our trust in AI systems.

The Tamil poet Valluvar wrote about wisdom in 500 CE, which is frequently translated as, "The wise with watchful soul who imminent ills foresee; from the forthcoming evil's dreaded shock are free." We can ameliorate the shock and surprise of the "big one" for AI if we are willing to wise up about the brittleness of AI. Whether AI's future story is one of how wisely we used this time to proactively shore up resources to protect high-stakes AI systems or how we ignored the warnings of our modern-day Paul Reveres and Rachel Carsons depends largely on the investments we make today. Invest today in awareness. Demand security today. By doing so, you choose the compelling but carefully vetted and proactively protected AI systems for tomorrow. To redound or reject these early warnings, to stand or fall, free in our own arbitrament, it lies.

So, with providence as our guide, let us walk, hand in hand, in the garden of forking paths.

Appendix A
Big-Picture Questions

1 0-701 is the registration code for the machine learning class at Carnegie Mellon University. I took this class purely at my graduate advisor's goading, who wanted me to "look beyond" computer security. I remember my advisor saying, "Tom wrote the textbook on ML, and you will pick up something from him; give the class a chance." So, for two days a week for an entire semester in 2011, I filed into the always-chilly auditorium with 50 other students into Wean Hall, CMU's ugliest, brutalist building, to hear the ML virtuoso, Tom Mitchell. This class set in motion a decade-long obsession with combining computer security and machine learning.

In lieu of recapping all the lectures at the end of the semester, Mitchell shared the five big-picture questions about machine learning that he carries in his head. His rationale was that if you knew what questions to ask when confronted with a new ML algorithm, you could pretty much get its gist. Whenever I read a landmark paper in machine learning, these big-picture questions have played Virgil to my Dante.

In that spirit, Hyrum and I are providing five questions that we encourage business executives, policymakers, and engineering managers to ask teams building and deploying ML systems. On their face, these questions are not earth-shattering. But they serve as a useful tool to begin important conversations about your organization's security posture for ML systems.

As ML continues to proliferate, everyone—governments, organizations, and consumers—must proactively think about their security.

If you run into problems or need help, please get in touch at notwithabug@ram-shankar.com. I care deeply about the intersection of machine learning and security, and it is important we get this right.

—Ram Shankar

Question to Ask	What to Look For
What are the risks to the consumer and the organization if an adversary could corrupt or directly control the output of the machine learning system?	✓ The team has identified the "crown jewels" of their ML systems and knows what can go wrong.
Can you walk me through your machine learning system's threat model?	✓ The team has mapped adversary capabilities to tamper with training data, test data, and the algorithm.
What safeguards are in place that raise the cost of an attack against our ML systems?	The team has taken precautionary measures to: ✓ Build the ML system using the best traditional and adversarial ML security practices. ✓ Robustly test the ML system and third-party software and data dependencies before deployment. ✓ Monitor model behavior and user interactions after deployment.

Question to Ask	What to Look For
Let's assume the system has been compromised. How will you know if an attack on the ML system has occurred?	✓ The organization has an owner for AI security. ✓ The team has instrumented its software and data ingestion pipelines, training pipelines, deployment pipelines, and inference systems with logging and/or attack detection capabilities.
What is our response plan when the ML system is attacked?	✓ The team has a viable fallback plan when the ML system is compromised that might include human override controls.

Acknowledgments

To paraphrase Milton, the subject of this book pleased me, long choosing and beginning late. It was my pandemic sourdough, but it would still be just unleavened flour and water without the contributions of so many.

Collaborating with Hyrum on the book was the easiest decision I have ever made. Diomedes, said it best, when he picked the all powerful Ulysses as his companion for a quest: "When two men are together, one of them may see some opportunity which the other has not caught sight of; if a man is alone he is less full of resource, and his wit is weaker." Hyrum is an adversarial ML researcher non pareil, all powerful, ever kind, and I am grateful, like Diomedes, for having Hyrum on this journey and making my wit stronger in the process.

David Fugate is the stuff of legends in the literary world. In my friend's immortal words, "How on Earth do you and Andy Weir have the same agent?" I honestly don't know. What I do know is that David's superpower is listening. At every turn, David would hear our questions, thoughtfully analyze the situation, proceed to provide an unseen perspective, and then navigate the situation like a consummate professional. He is a superstar, and we are lucky he is in our orbit.

Jim Minatel, our editor at Wiley, shaped this book with intention and care. He nudged us, challenged us, guided us at every turn, and coaxed the best in us. Hyrum and I are grateful to Jim for his omnidirectional leadership; to Rick Kugen, for his keen eye; and to the entire Wiley team for getting this book out.

Just like it took a team of three to revive Schubert's *Symphony No. 9* and three chefs to bring French cooking across the Atlantic, it took a team of three to deliver this book. Russell Thacker, our indefatigable de facto first-round copy editor, deserves every bit of Hyrum and mine's immortal garland. He did so much more than copy edit. Russell had the odious job of reading our first drafts with dangling participles, unfinished thoughts, jumbled logic, and unnecessary pop culture allusions. Like the editors of Alexandria working their way through Homer, not only did he lop, prune, prop, and bind our writing, but he also provided the first eye, giving editorial feedback, organizing, and immeasurably improving our manuscript.

David Cross was the first to read the book cover to cover. Anyone who has worked with David knows he is not only a sterling security leader but also an expansive reader. You can count on David to provide an honest yet nourishing assessment of any situation. So, like a home inspector surveying a townhome, he pointed out where the manuscript leaked and where it was adequately fortified—all in peerless email response times. After patching these proverbial holes, Hyrum and I turned the crank again, sending it to a fresh batch of readers. This time, we benefited from Ryan Middleton and Drew Lohn, who provided further guidance on getting the content and context right.

So much happens after the manuscript is done. Hyrum and I are particularly grateful to Vikram Ravi Ramanathan, who helped us marshal our book launch plan. Vikram is a brand whisperer and a marketing maven. Hyrum and I benefited from the punctilious plan he laid out, his masterful execution, and his incessant cheerleading.

Subsequently, the book went through numerous rewrites and revisions, thanks to the feedback and conversations with experts across the spectrum ranging from AI researchers, cybersecurity professionals, policy wonks, and business leaders: Kendra Albert, Ross Anderson, Mayuran Athimoolam, Ylli Bajraktari, John Bansemer, Battista Biggio, Harold Booth, Miles Brundage, Andrew Burt, Nicholas Carlini, Jason Chan, Kamalika Chaudhury, Maggie Delano, eric douglas, Oren Etzioni, David Evans, Ivan Evtimov, Kevin Eykholt, Adam Fuchs, Ryan Fedasiuk, Earlence Fernandes, Nate Fick, Nic Fillingham, David Freeman, Tom Goldstein, Ian Goodfellow, Kathrin Grosse, Maya Gupta, Dan Hendrycks, Srinivasan Iyer, Ann Johnson, Frank Nagle, Sudipto Rakshit, Yoshi Kohno, Hima Lakkaraju, Mark McGovern, Nicolas Papernot, Will Pearce, Brian Pendleton, Jon Penney, Jane Pinelis, Asfaneh Rigot, Mikel Rodriguez, Abhishek Shivakumar, Vasavi Sundaram, (thank you, Sesame!) Paul Scharre, Bruce Schneier, Giorgio Severi, Matt Swann, Christian Szegedy, Helen Toner, Florian Tramèr, and Chris Wysopal. This book stands on their shoulders.

I am profoundly beholden to Mark Russinovich, Eric Horvitz and Matt Swann's mentorship. Titans in their fields, they teach me in each interaction to be curious and challenge my own assumptions about how the world works. This book would not be possible without their kindness and generosity.

I am also thankful to PJ Maykish, Mikel Rodriguez, Sharon Xia, Hyrum Anderson, Ryan Kovar, and Nicolas Papernot for playing Aeolus to my Odysseus. They truly sparkle in their generosity.

Entwined during the pandemic was my own *arkhê kakôn*. But thanks to my brother and my rock, Imran Kadher Mastan, and my *modhal kattam* I found the courage to hurl myself into the abyss and discover it's a feather bed.

The book is also a paean to the Pacific Northwest. It was written in the unceded ancestral land of the indigenous people who are still here. When the inspiration to write responded to my calls with a mortifying negative, I found solace, succor, and solitude in the beauty around me. From the Anacortes Islands to the Alpine Wilderness lakes; from the mountains of Snoqualmie to the meadows of Summerland; from the sunrises in Port Ludlow to the sundowns in Mukilteo; from Cougar Mountain's slopes to Ada Technical Café's armchair; from King FM's Morning Shot of Musical espresso to Winthrop morning runs—all pugnaciously pulled away the tyranny of the blank page and playfully poured forth the panache of a magniloquent spoony. I am Madras at heart and Evergreen in soul.

Ram Shankar

Index

A

Accept Cookies button, 144–145
active deception, 114
adversarial example
    algorithms and, 116–117
    attacker goal regarding, 111
    characteristics of, 130
    on clothing, 60–61, 79–80
    cost of, 80
    defense challenges regard-
        ing, 108–111
    detection of, 130
    discovery of, 60, 63, 77
    existence and func-
        tion of, 66–70
    impact of, 80
    in military, 82
    neural network and,
        107–108

numbers as, 68–69
    overtrust of, 80
    overview of, 59–62
    parameter adjustment of,
        72
    response to threats of, 113
    tools regarding, 81
adversarial machine learning
    adjustments within, 73
    cargo cult science
        within, 156–157
    example of, 44–45
    legal implications of,
        72–73
    overview of, ii, 18, 20
    security and machine learn-
        ing fields and, 63–64
adversarial mindset, 132
adversarial retraining, 130–131

adversary. *See also* attacker
  characteristics of, 80, 164
  collective, 21
  defined, 20, 59, 101, 109
  examples of, 109
  game theory and, 64
  goal of, 63, 81
  mindset of, 132
  types of, 88
  worst-case scenario strategy
    regarding, 128
advertising, 101, 102
African Americans, incarcera-
    tion of, 148
Albert, Kendra (scholar), 72–73
Alexa, 81, 82, 91–92, 94–95
"Alexa for Artillery," 13
AlexNet, 34
algorithm
  adversarial examples
    and, 116–117
  advertising, 101
  building, 88
  for computer vision, 32–33
  data format for, 88–89
  dataset errors and, 90–91
  of Google, 97
  gradient descent, 71–72
  k-nearest neighbor, 77–78
  poisoning attack on, 104–105
  random-forest, 77–78
  search engine failures of, 95–96
  support vector machine, 77–78
  vulnerability of, 104
algorithmic disgorgement, 157
Algorithmic Justice League, 20

Alpha G AI, 3
Amazon Mechanical Turk, 89
AMD, 169
American College Testing
    (ACT) Test, 77
American Medical Collection
    Agency (AMCA), 172
Anderson, Ross (profes-
    sor), 137–138
antimalware system, poisoning
    attack on, 148
antivirus, subscriptions
    to, 124–125
Apple, 119–124, 169
Arabic language, 42–43, 126–127
Area 52, 10–12
Army Engineering University
    (China), 26
artificial intelligence (AI).
    See also machine
    learning (ML)
  Achilles' heel of, 25–28
  advancement rate of, 3
  as arms race, 174
  "big one" regarding,
    166–169, 172–173
  business at the speed of, 2–4
  confidence in, i–ii
  defined, 2
  failure causes of, 29–30
  Great Acceleration of, ii
  high switching costs
    regarding, 139
  human understanding
    regarding, 9
  illiteracy regarding, 9, 164

internal use of, 124
marketing regarding, 8–9
mutual benefits of, 139
overtrust of, 6–10, 54
overview of, i–ii
policies regarding, iii–iv
as software 2.0, 166
undevelopment of, 135
up-front investment
    in, 138–139
winner takes all dynamic
    regarding, 138–140
Artificial Intelligence Act
    (AIA), 144–145,
    149, 154, 172
assessment, 141–144,
    145, 151–152
assume-breach mindset, 129
AsuharietYgvar, 121
Athalye, Anish
    (researcher), 117
attacker. *See also* adversary
    AI interface by, 17
    challenge of, 17–18
    characteristics of, 108, 164
    defined, 109
    first movers' advantage
        of, 109–110
    goal of, 18, 111
    misleading, 114
    motivation for, 82
    odds regarding, 24
    romanticized view of, 164
    surrogate model con-
        trol by, 118
    types of, 108–109

Austin, Lloyd (U.S. Army
    General), 25
autonomous vehicle. *See* self-
    driving cars

B
bad data, 87–88
Bajraktari, Ylli (NSCAI leader-
    ship), 12–16
banking, 78, 93, 146
bargain bin model, 75–79, 119
Bengio, Yoshua (AI pioneer), 57
BERT (Google), 93–94
bias, within machine learning
    (ML), 148–149
"big one" mindset, 166–169,
    172–173
Biggio, Battista (researcher),
    63–64, 65, 104, 118
Bing (Microsoft), 46, 97–99
black box attack
    bail and, 147
    bargain bin model of, 119
    as consequential, 79
    defined, 76–77
    example of, 112–113
    process of, 81
    transferability prop-
        erty and, 78
    types of, 112
BlenderBot 3 (Meta), 22
blind reliance, 4–6
Blumenthal, Richard (U.S.
    Senator), 120
boundary decision, 68–69
Bradley, Phelim (Prolific), 86

breach, data, 167–168, 172
Bridle, James
    (researcher), 49–50
Brussels effect, 144–145
bug bounty, 116
Buolamwini, Joy
    (scholar), 27, 149
Burger King, 37–38
Burris, Ethan (professor), 108
business, 2–4, 47–48

C
Canada, 13, 67–68
CardSystems Solutions, 168
cargo cult science, 156–157
Carlini, Nicholas (researcher),
    115–118, 130, 156–157
CE (conformité européenne)
    marking, 141
Central Intelligence Agency
    (CIA), 126
certification, AI, 144
Chief Digital and Artificial
    Intelligence Office
    (CDAO), 165
child safety measures, 120
child sexual abuse material
    (CSAM), 120, 121
China
    as AI's Achilles' heel, 25–28
    antivirus research of, 125
    data breach by, 168
    diplomacy with, 175
    social media usage by, 26
    threat regarding, 174
Clarifai, 31

clickstream, 98–99
clothing, adversarial examples
    of, 60–61, 79–80
Common Crawl, 93
communication, encryption
    within, 23–24
comprehensive testing, 141
computer gaming, 34
computer processing
    unit (CPU), 34
computer vision. See also image
    algorithm for, 32–33
    color and shape overreliance
        within, 39–40
    cropped image misinterpreta-
        tion by, 123
    decomposition limita-
        tions of, 36
    distortion and, 39–40
    glass viewing by, 39–40
    hue and saturation changes
        to, 51, 52
    limitations of, 35
    progress within, 31–32
    rotated image misinterpreta-
        tion by, 52–53, 123
    unexpected object misinter-
        pretation by, 52
confidence, 23, 113, 114
confidentiality, attacks
    regarding, 112
Consumer Electronic Show, 119
consumer products, manu-
    facturer requirements
    regarding, 141

convolutional neural network (CNN), 32–33
Conway's Law, 165
copyright infringement, 99–100, 170–171
Cordon, James (television personality), 10
Cornelius, Cory (researcher), 123
counter AI. *See* adversarial machine learning
COVID-19 pandemic, 6–7, 27, 131
cyber army (Ukraine), 102
Cyber Grand Challenge, 17
cyber insurance, 143
cyber pandemic, 171
cybersecurity, 109–111, 125
Cybersecurity and Infrastructure Security Agency (CISA), 27

D
Darby, Chris (In-Q-Tel CEO), 172
DARPA, 17, 18, 177
data breach, 167–168, 172
data labeler, 89–90
data quality management, 87–88
data/dataset. *See also* input data
  annotating of, 89, 90–91
  derived, 93
  errors within, 90, 91
  images within, 30–31
  large-scale, 31

machine learning (ML) prediction regarding, 36
open source, 89
refining of, 88–89
unannotated, 92
deception, active, 114
decision boundary, 68–69
deep learning, 34, 76
deep neural network, 34, 77–78
deepfake, 18
Deepmind, 3
defense in depth, 131–132
Department of Defense (DoD), 133, 134–135
Desiigner, 99
detector-with-model, 130
digital watermarking, 100
DNNResearch, 31
"Drag *vs.* AI" workshop, 20
drugs, 12

E
Easterly, Jen (CISA director), 171
email, spam within, 63
encryption, within communication, 23–24
error gradient, 72
Evans, David (professor), 23
Evtimov, Ivan (sign holder), 1, 28, 30
explainability property, 148
Exum, Andrew (Middle East deputy assistant secretary of defense), 12
Eykholt, Kevin (student), 30

F

Facebook, 21, 40, 42–44, 89, 101–102

facial recognition, 20, 61, 77, 149–151

Fake Contacts 2, 102

Fedasiuk, Ryan (research analyst), 26

Federal Aviation Administration (FAA), 126

Federal Security Service (FSB) (Russia), 168

Feynman, Richard (physicist), 156

FIFA, 2

fine-tuning, 92

flight-or-fight situation, blind reliance within, 5–6

Flournoy, Michèle (Under Secretary of Defense for Policy), 135

ForAllSecure, 17

Form 10-K, 154

Frank, Sarah (influencer), 85

Fridman, Lex (podcaster), 107–108

full-knowledge attack, 76

G

Game of Thrones, 45

game theory, 64

Gebru, Timnit (scholar), 27, 149

gender, experiment regarding, 147–148

General Data Protection Regulation (GDPR), 144–145, 154

General Motors, 177

generative adversarial network (GAN), 65

Genius, 99–100, 102

ghost worker, 88–91

glasses, adversarial examples of, 61, 79–80

Glenn, John (U.S. Senator), 176

global positioning system (GPS), 46–47

Gmail, spamming on, 100–101

Go board game, 3

Go Fish game, 73

Goldberg, Ian (professor), 116

Goodfellow, Ian (author), 57–59, 62, 64, 65, 108

Google

 AI system of, 3

 algorithm of, 97

 BERT, 93–94

 business faking within, 47–48

 copyright infringement case of, 99–100, 102

 deep learning research of, 76

 employee perks of, 57–58

 lyric searching within, 99–100

 machine learning engineer style guide of, 104–105

 plagiarism case of, 97

 search failure of, 95

 text processing system of, 62

Google bombing, 46

Google Home speaker, 81
Google Maps, 8, 46–47
Google Translate, 43
GoRando, 102
Gordon, Sue (ODNI leader-
    ship), 127–128
Gotleib, Scott (FDA commis-
    sioner), 53
gradient descent, 71–72, 77, 78,
    113–114, 118
gradient masking, 113, 118–119
graphics processing
    unit (GPU), 34
Gray, Mary (anthropologist), 89
guns, scanners for, 38

H
handwriting, machine recogni-
    tion of, 67, 78
hash, 120
Hendrycks, Dan
    (researcher), 35
Hicks, Kathleen (Deputy Secre-
    tary of Defense), 25
high-stakes decision, AI usage
    within, 146–147
Hinton, Geoffrey (educator), 76
Homendy, Jennifer (National
    Transportation Safety
    Board), 155
honeypot word, 98, 102
Horvitz, Eric (Microsoft
    Chief Scientific
    Officer), 162–163
House Armed Services
    Committee, 14

Howard, Ayanna (professor), 5
hue (color), changes to, 51, 52
Huebner, Ben (ODNI lead-
    ership), 129
human vision, 32, 35–36

I
IBM, 7–8
image. *See also* computer vision
    adversarial example of, 59–62
    annotating of, 89
    attacks regarding, 112
    black box attack example
        regarding, 112–113
    copyright infringement
        of, 170–171
    cropped, 123
    data labeling of, 89–90
    deviation challenges
        regarding, 66
    edge identification of, 32–33
    example of, 35, 39, 40, 41, 52,
        53, 56, 73, 74, 90, 103
    hue and saturation changes
        to, 51, 52
    medical image scan of, 70
    modifications of, 73
    NeuralHash usage
        of, 120–124
    noise pattern within, 69,
        73–74, 149, 150
    number changes within, 67–69
    parameters regarding, 71–72
    pertubations to, 58
    pixel color changes
        within, 58, 60

image. *See also* computer vision
(*continued*)
poisoning attack regarding, 103
rotated, 52–53, 123
as spam, 63
specific changes to, 56
subtle changes to, 56
ImageNet dataset
annotated images of, 89
data quality of, 36
error rate within, 34,
35, 39, 51
labeling errors within, 90, 91
overview of, 33
poster regarding, 30–31
winning algorithm of, 35
ImageNet Large Scale Visual
Recognition Challenge
(ILSVRC), 31–32
in medias res, 178–179
incarceration, 148
indirect cue, regarding race and
gender, 147–148
information asymmetry, 109–110
input data. *See also* data/dataset
within adversarial exam-
ple, 107, 111
corruption of, 87–88
game theory and, 59
image of, 72
inspection of, 60
poisoning attack of, 22, 100
prompting with, 112
of self-driving cars, 49
in whitebox gradient
attacks, 78

insecurity, causes of, 138
insider threat, 169
insurance, 142–143
intentional failure mode, 19–20
International Conference on
Learning Representa-
tions (ICLR), 117
Iraq, 125–126
Israel, surveillance technology of, 134

J
James, Jonathan (breacher),
167
JASON advisory group,
133, 134–135
Jennings, Ken (television
personality), 7
Jeopardy, 7
Joyce, Rob (NSA cybersecurity
director), 110
js13kGames, 115–118
justified confidence, 23

K
Karpathy, Andrej (Tesla director
of AI), 166
Kaspersky, 103
Kennedy, John F. (U.S. President), 175
keyword stuffing, 20–21
k-nearest neighbor algo-
rithm, 77–78
Kohno, Yoshi (student), 176
Krizhevsky, Alex
(researcher), 34

L

L0pht Heavy Industries, 159–160
Lakkaraju, Hima (professor), 146, 147–148
language, 42–44, 61–62, 91–92, 126–127
LeCun Net, 34
Li, Fei-Fei (professor), 30–31
Li, Tiffany C. (professor), 157
Lieberman, Joe (U.S. Senator), 178
Livdahl, Kristin (mother), 94
Log4j library, 171
Lohn, Andrew (Georgetown University, 26–27, 163
Lycée Louis-Le-Grand, 75
lyrics, copyright infringement of, 99–100, 102

M

machine learning (ML). *See also* artificial intelligence (AI)
  adversarial machine learning and, 63–64
  assumptions regarding, 20
  bias within, 148–149
  big-picture questions regarding, 181–183
  data prediction by, 36
  drugs and, 12
  failure of, 19–22
  faux construction of, 66
  function of, 2–3
  odds of breaking, 24

  as open-source, 74–75
  parameters of, 71–72, 74–75
  proliferation of, 4
  uses for, 4
Madry, Aleksander (professor), 117
MafiaBoy (breacher), 167–168
Magnuson Park, Seattle, Washington, 1
maps, manipulation of, 46–48
marketing, of artificial intelligence (AI), 8–9
masking, 111–114, 118–119
Mayhem (ForAllSecure), 17–18
McDaniel, Patrick (professor), 75–76
McGroddy, Kathy (IBM Watson Health), 8
medicine, 6–8, 53, 70, 146
membership inference attack, 112
Metamind, 31
Microsoft Windows 2000, 137, 138
military, 10–12, 82, 134
The Mitchells vs. the Machines (film), 29, 52
mobile gaming, 87
MobilEye sensor (Tesla), 48–49, 51
model inversion attack, 112
model stealing (model extraction) attack, 78, 112
Mozilla, 101
Mueller, Robert (FBI director), 126–127

multifactor authentication
(MFA), 142–143
Munroe, Randall (author), 170
Murphy's Law, 164
Musk, Elon (Tesla
CEO), 107–108

N
National Defense Authoriza-
tion Act, 164
National Defense Univer-
sity, 12–13
National Geospatial-
Intelligence Agency
(NGA), 128
National Highway Traffic
Safety Administration
(NTHSA), 177
National Institute of Stand-
ards and Technology
(NIST), 67, 144
National Security Commission
on Artificial Intelligence
(NSCAI), 14–18, 22–23,
28, 82, 163
National Security
Council, 13–14
natural language processing
(NLP), 91–92
navigation, 8, 46–48
Neural Information Process-
ing Systems (NeurIPS),
62–63, 137
neural network, 57–60,
107–108, 135
NeuralHash (Apple), 120–124

noise pattern, 69, 73–74, 149, 150
numbers, machine recogni-
tion of, 67–69
nuTonomy, 36–37
Nvidia, 154, 169

O
obfuscation, 101, 113
O'Brien, Mary (Deputy Chief of
Staff), 83
offensive AI, 17
Office of Director of
National Intelligence
(ODNI), 126–129
open-source intelligence
(OSINT), 110
open-source software, 170, 171
Oprea, Alina (profes-
sor), 104, 148
organizational structure, failures regarding, 165
Our Community Now, 94–95
output, adversary goal
regarding, 72
overtrust, 6–10, 54, 80,
94–96, 155

P
panda/gibbon image, 56, 59-60,
64, 112-113, 149
Papernot, Nicholas (researcher),
75–79, 118, 135
parameters, of machine learning (ML), 71–72
Pearl, Judea (Turing Award
winner), 9

penny challenge, 94–95
Pentagon, 11, 12, 13
people of color, facial recognition limitations regarding, 149–150
perception, standards and, 142
Perlroth, Nicole (reporter), 102
Permissive Action Links (PAL), 175
Pinelis, Jane (Department of Defense), 22–23
pixel, alteration of, 58, 60
plagiarism, 97–99
poisoning attack, 22, 87–88, 96–103, 104–105, 148
policy, artificial intelligence (AI), iii–iv
Pompeo, Mike (Secretary of State), 26
pornography, social media flagging of, 40–41, 51
Potter, Stewart (U.S. Supreme Court Justice), 42
Powell, Colin (Secretary of State), 126
prevention-focused manager, 108
privacy, 119–124
proem, 16
Prolific, 86
promotion-focused manager, 108

R
race, experiment regarding, 147–148
Raji, Deborah (scholar), 27, 149

random-forest algorithm, 77–78
ransomware attack, 169
Recorded Futures, 125
red team, 11, 163
Reddit, 45
research survey, 85–86
ResNet, 34
@ResNextGuesser, 36
Rigler, Tara (Department of the Interior), 15
risk, reality of, 128
risk management framework (AI), 144
robotic assistant, 4–6
Rodriguez, Mikel (Area 52), 10–11
Russia, 4, 18, 27, 134
Russian Defense Ministry, 82

S
Samuel, Arthur (AI pioneer), 2
saturation (color intensity), changes to, 51, 52
Savage, Stefan (student), 176
ScanEagle, 11
Schmidt, Eric (Google CEO), 12, 14
Scholastic Aptitude Test (SAT), 77
schools, AI scanners within, 38
search engines, 45–46, 95, 97–99, 101
security
    advantages regarding, 174
    adversarial machine learning and, 63–64

security (*continued*)
  adversarial mindset
    regarding, 132
  Apple and, 119–124
  awareness of, 164
  "big one" regarding, 166–
    169, 172–173
  black box attack and, 79
  causes against, 138
  demand for, 179–180
  importance of, 136–140
  information asymmetry
    within, 109–110
  mentality regarding, 167
  obscurity and, 124–125
  preparation statistics regard-
    ing, 161–162
  public opinion regarding, 173
  punting of, 140
  race to, 173–176
  risk tolerance within, 153
  safe/unsafe thinking
    within, 153
  standards regarding, 141–144
security risk assessment, 132
seizure, 95
self-driving cars
  adversarial machine learning
    regarding, 18
  failures of, 81
  input of, 49
  insider threat regarding, 169
  line interpretation of, 49–50
  within the military, 135
  misrecognition by, 37–38
  nuTonomy, 36–37

  overtrust in, 9–10
  projection sensitivity of, 50
  security of, 177
  speed manipulation
    regarding, 48–51
  weather affecting, 37
Shane, Janelle (author), 19
shared creation, 129
shattered gradient, 114
Shum, Harry (Microsoft
    Search), 97
Singhal, Amit (Google
    Search), 98
skin, AI use regarding, 2
smart speaker, 81–82, 89–90,
    94–96, 138–139
smart system, adversarial exam-
    ples of, 61
Smashwords, 93
social bias, within machine
    learning (ML), 148–149
social media, 26
software, challenges regard-
    ing, 169–171
Song, Dawn (professor), 132
Soviet Union, 175
spamming, 63, 100–101
speech recognition, 12
speed limit, manipula-
    tion of, 48–51
Squires, Marak (devel-
    oper), 170–171
standards, security, 141–144,
    152–153, 154
stochastic gradient, 113–114
stop sign, 1–2, 29–30, 55

Stratego, 3
support vector machine, 77–78
surface-to-surface missiles, 19
surrogate model, 78–79, 118
surveillance, 134
survey, research, 85–86
Sutskever, Ilya (author), 57, 64
switching cost, 139
Syrian war, 134
systems approach manager,
      108
Szegedy, Cristian (author), 57,
      58–59, 62, 64, 77

T
Tay (Microsoft), 21–22, 88, 110
Tenenbaum, Joshua
      (professor), 9
Tesla
   crashes involving, 81
   data labelers of, 89, 91
   exaggeration of, 155
   insider threat of, 169
   limitations of, 37–38
   safety ratings of, 155
   speed manipulation
      regarding, 48–51
testing, 141–144, 145, 151–152
text processing, adversarial
      examples of, 61–62
text-based system, fallibil-
      ity of, 20–21
Theroux, Louis (documen-
      tarian), 19
Thompson, Fred (U.S. Senator),
      159, 160, 161, 166, 173

Thompson, Ken (Turing Award
      winner), 170
Toner, Helen (Georgetown Uni-
      versity), 174
Track THIS, 101
transferability property, 78–79
translation, failures
      regarding, 42–44
Trump, Donald (U.S. Presi-
      dent), 16, 25
trust, 7, 8–9, 23
Tumblr, 40–41, 51
Twitter, 21–22, 26, 40–41
typo, for AI evasion, 21

U
Ukraine/Ukraine War,
      4, 18, 102
unannotated data, 92
Underwriters Laborato-
      ries (UL), 141
unintentional failure, 19
Unit 61398 (China), 168
Unity, 87
University of Hertfordshire, 4–6
University of Mary-
      land, 149–150
University of Toronto, 32–33
unsupervised learning,
      advancement in, 92
U.S. Air Force, 19

V
Valluvar (poet), 179
vampire novels, AI empower-
      ment by, 93–94

Vanuatu, 156
Varian, Hal (professor), 137–138
video gaming, 115–118
VirusTotal, 103
vulnerability, 104, 111, 162

W
Wagner, David (professor), 116
Waldman, Ari Ezra (author), 164–165
Walker, Mike (ForAllSecure), 17
Walla Walla onion, Facebook misflagging of, 40
Watson Health, 7–8
weapons, 27, 38
weather, self-driving cars and, 37
websites
  deepfakesweb, 18
  Nicolas.Carlini, 115
  Not with a Bug But with a Sticker, iii
  Smashwords, 93
  Wikipedia, 92
WeChat, 43–44

Weckert, Simon (navigation manipulator), 46–47
white-box attack, 76, 78, 118
wiggle-jiggle, intelligent, 71–75
Wikipedia, 92–93, 100
winner takes all dynamic, of artificial intelligence (AI), 138–140
World War II, 156
Wysopal, Chris (hacker), 172–173

X
XPeng, 169

Y
Yahoo!, 168
Yandex Taxi (Russia), 169

Z
Zaremba, Wojciech "Woj" (researcher), 58
Zelensky, Volodymyr (Ukraine President), 18
zero-knowledge attack, 76–77
Zhora, Victor, 102